FROM PICASSO
TO JEFF KOONS

The artist
as jeweler

EDITED BY
DIANE VENET

The question of style has been fundamental throughout the history of jewelry. For this reason we have chosen to organize and present objects by category and not necessarily according to chronological periods.

DIANE VENET WOULD LIKE TO THANK:

THE PHOTOGRAPHERS:

Luis Asin,
Schana B Gallery,
Yann Delacour,
Alexandre Devals,
Benjamin Didier,
Grégory Favre,
Peter Frese,
Sherry Griffin,
Philippe Gontier,
Angela Larotonda,
Alain LePrince,
Brian Moghadam,
Mark Niedermann,
Thomas Trangle

THE AMERICAN LENDERS:

Naomi Antonakos,
Corice Arman,
Sara and Marc Benda,
James Brown,
Audrey Friedman,
Patricia Pastor Friedman,
Rosalind Jacobs,
Ilya and Emilia Kabakov,
Bill Katz,
Sofia LeWitt,
Roy Lichtenstein Foundation,
Pace Wildenstein Gallery,
Barbara Rose,
Keith Sonnier,
Frank Stella,
Donald Sultan Studio,
Barbara Tober

THE EUROPEAN LENDERS:

Margareta Von Bartha,
Stephanie Busuttil,
Elisabetta Cipriani,
Pierre-Alain Challier,
Princesse Michael of Greece,
Louisa Guinness,
Marie Haddou,
Didier and Martine Haspeslagh
+ Didier Antiques,
Éclipse,
Marina Filippini,
Cornelia Fourneau de Mello,
Mourao,
Ingrid Jochheim,
Diana Küppers,
Museo Chillida-Leku,
Grassy Madrid
and Sir Anthony Caro,
Sheila van der Marck,
Germana Matta,
Naïla de Monbrison,
Ursula Painvin,
Irmgard Rademacher,
Elisabeth Royer,
Berenice de Roquemaurel,
Christian Scheffel,
Natalie Seroussi,
Bernar Venet

AND PARTICULAR THANKS TO:

Barbara Rose
Deborah Laks
Esther de Beaucé
Audrey Lea Collins
Camille Giordano
Delphine Seïté
Plum Le Tan
Bernar Venet Studio

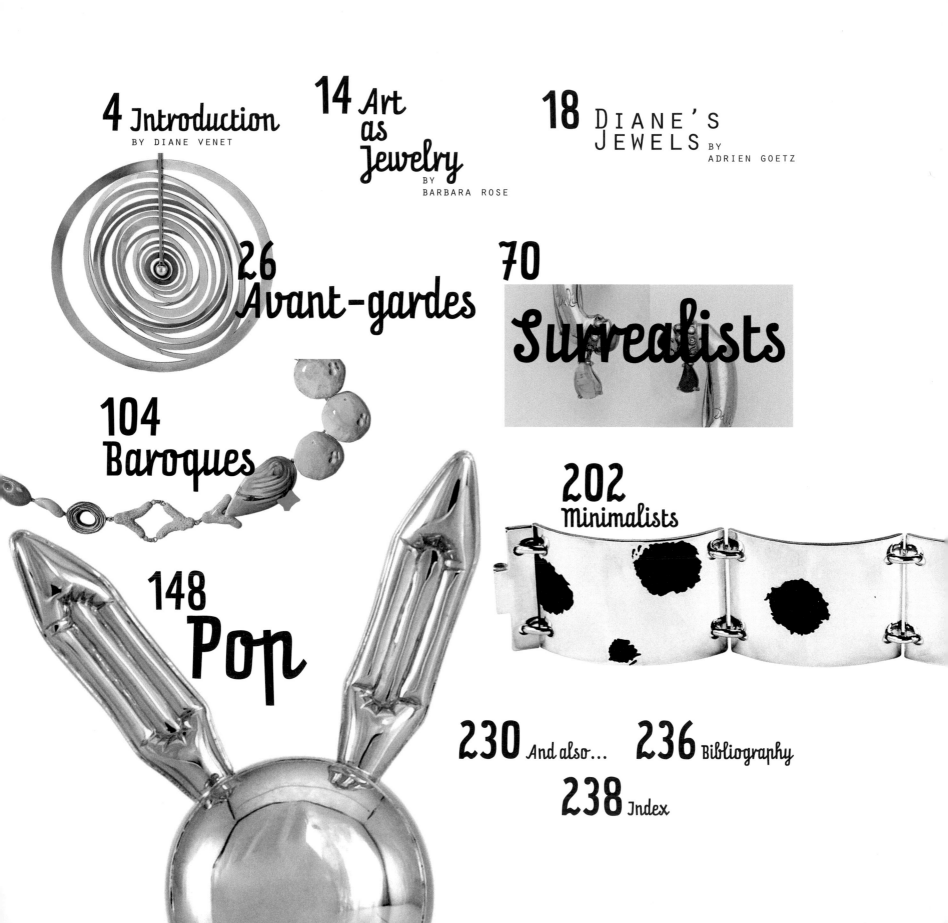

4 Introduction
BY DIANE VENET

14 Art as Jewelry
BY BARBARA ROSE

18 DIANE'S JEWELS BY ADRIEN GOETZ

26 Avant-gardes

70 Surrealists

104 Baroques

148 Pop

202 Minimalists

230 And also...   **236** Bibliography

238 Index

Introductio

BY DIANE VENET

In my rather itinerant life, my collection of jewelry is thus an intimate museum that I can take everywhere with me, and the treasure trove which I can find on my return home. I often arrange them in an "installation" or in "scenographies" that I can rearrange according to my mood of the moment and my pleasure in displaying them. But I also enjoy bringing out my different pieces from their jewelry boxes in order to expose them to the eyes of the collector.

Man Ray, *Portrait de Dora Maar*, 1936
Photomontage, 9 7/16 x 11 13/16 in. (24 x 30 cm)
Private collection

THE SPECTATOR CANNOT FAIL TO BE MOVED, DISCOVERING SIMULTANEOUSLY THE DUAL STAMP OF GENIUS AND LOVER.

Jewelry-making and artistic creation share a long and intimately interwoven history. It was only in the sixteenth century that their paths began to separate. Painters and sculptors began to be categorized as artists, while goldsmiths, despite their virtuosity, continued to be considered as craftsmen. From then on, the disciplines evolved independently, developing their own technical innovations and forging their separate histories. By the twentieth century, the division between the two types of production seemed insuperable. Visual arts embraced the immaterial, the ephemeral, and the conceptual, characteristics which seemed quite foreign to the domain of jewelry. The jewelry-maker meanwhile was driven by the demands of his materials, the value of his work being measured more often than not in carats.

Here, however, is a different story about jewelry, far from the shiny pages of the glossy magazines. It is the story of various distinguished artists, both male and female, who became interested in this adventure, inspired variously by love for wife or daughter, by the challenge, or simply out of interest for this particular medium of expression.

My passion for artists' jewelry was born on the day Bernar amused himself by rolling a thin stick of silver around my left ring finger to make me a wedding ring.... This first gesture, so moving in its spontaneity, had a far-reaching impact on me. It allowed me to discover the scarcely known universe of such unique and precious works of art. Precious not simply because of their rarity, but also for the symbolic content that is often at the origin of their creation.

Mimmo Rotella, slashed poster framed as a jewel,
for Diane Venet, 1996
Raymond Hains, composition to frame and wear as a jewel,
for Diane Venet, 1998

At a time when work made to order is becoming increasingly rare, artists' jewelry seems to be an exception. A piece may be created as an edition of several examples (usually around ten), but it has often been realized with a particular person in mind. The link created by the relationship between the artist and the beneficiary of his work is doubtless one of the main reasons for the fascination exerted by this type of jewelry. In the pebbles which Picasso collected on the beach and then painted for Dora Maar, or on the pieces of bone on which he engraved the portrait of his partner Marie-Thérèse, the intensity of his passion is tethered to his artistic gesture, and the spectator cannot fail to be moved, discovering simultaneously the dual stamp of genius and lover.

These miniature works of art, conceived for a loved one and intended for a very select market of connoisseurs, also give many artists the opportunity to test their practical ability and to confront unprecedented constraints. Bernar, entering into the spirit of things, followed up

Robert Indiana, certificate for the *Love* ring
For Diane Venet, 2003

the creation of the wedding ring with brooches and bracelets. Each one corresponded to a new concept in his artistic activity. I thus possess an exhaustive and representative collection of jewelry that corresponds to the *Indeterminate Lines*, *Arcs*, *Angles*, and *Straight Lines* which have made up his artistic vocabulary for the past few years. Jacques Villeglé recently made me a ring that closely resembles his current work using his unique socio-political alphabet. Frank Stella created a titanium necklace for me, using his computer in the same way as when he makes his sculptures. Kader Attia designed a ring in the shape of handcuffs that attach two fingers together. Orlan created a perfect miniaturization of her self-portrait from the series African Self-hybridizations, and Pierrette Bloch an extension of her sculptural work. All these works constitute a miniature museum that can be worn on the wrist, the neck, or the finger. They offer a new appreciation of creations by some of the most important artists from the second half of the twentieth century and the twenty-first century, by confronting their plastic vocabulary with the inevitable changes necessary for their work to evolve into a piece of jewelry: size, weight, portability. Not exhaustive, but dictated by my own preferences and my personal interest in the work of certain artists, this collection is just like my passion for its creation: multi-form, playful, and exacting. In my rather itinerant life, my collection of jewelry is thus an intimate museum that I can take everywhere with me, and the treasure trove which I can find on my return home. I often arrange them in an "installation" or in "scenographies" that I can rearrange according to my mood of the moment and my pleasure in displaying them. But I also enjoy bringing out my different pieces from their jewelry boxes in order to expose them to the eyes of the collector. The exhibitions which I devise, yesterday in Roubaix, today in New York, tomorrow in Athens, and so on to many other major cities, allow me to show to the general public works which I love and appreciate. Because they recount a rather special history of art, made of exclusivity and passion, these works occupy a particular place in a museum. At first sight, nothing distinguishes them from the concentrated formulae of the sculptures from which they are derived. But their reason for being, as well as their destination, their dimension, and even the closeness to a woman's body that they represent, makes each one of them a special object.

All these pieces of jewelry have been conceived to be worn, even if some of them are ephemeral or particularly delicate. When I choose one of them from my collection for a

BECAUSE THEY RECOUNT
A RATHER SPECIAL
HISTORY OF ART,
MADE OF EXCLUSIVITY
AND PASSION,
THESE WORKS OCCUPY
A PARTICULAR PLACE
IN A MUSEUM.

THE BORDER BETWEEN THEM IS SUBTLE, AND THE WIFE OF AN ARTIST KNOWS ALL TOO WELL HOW POROUS IT CAN BE. I COLLECT DESIGNS, BUT ALSO NARRATIVES OF LIFE.

special occasion, I am always extremely sensitive to its closeness to me, to its intimate relation with art. I may roll a Takis around my wrist, or see myself reflected in a Kapoor around my neck. By wearing them, I offer them to be viewed by other people. Not only is there the pleasure of associating closely with them, but also that of letting other people look at them. I become, in a way, a torchbearer. The passage from muse to bearer brings to light all the facets of support which a woman who is loved, who is alternately collector, interlocutor, and inspirer, can offer to an artist. Female artists are also the originators of jewelry, of course. In the twentieth century, jewelry was a popular form of expression for female artists. The academic interest presented by these miniature works is augmented by the pleasure of being able to wear one's own work. Niki de Saint Phalle is notable in this category: her sense of color and composition was reflected in her choice of outfits and the dialogue she created between fabrics and enamels. The many pieces of jewelry that she created reflect closely the evolution of her work, and allow a relationship with her artistic creation that is harder to achieve with her sculptures which tend to overawe in their dimensions. A *Nana* worn on the lapel becomes an eloquent witness, just like all Saint Phalle's work, to a flamboyant and complex femininity. In the same way, one of Louise Bourgeois's spiders, when fixed to the collar of a coat, while losing none of its disturbing presence, seems to be tamed. Meret Oppenheim, Louise Nevelson, Jenny Holzer, and Kiki Smith are among other female artists who extended their plastic vocabulary into the domain of jewelry-making.

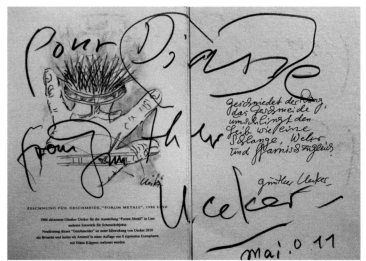

Günther Uecker, certificate for the *Untitled* ring for Diane Venet, 2011

I often meet women and men who share my interest in the jewelry designed by artists, a genuine community of its champions. There are several of us who will track a rare piece from country to country. They include Martine and Didier Haspeslagh, British collectors and dealers, both curious and also learned; Louisa Guinness, of course, who commissions work from various English artists ranging from Anish Kapoor to Anthony Gormley, from Michael Craig-Martin to Marc Quinn or Sam Taylor-Wood; and Diana Küppers, in Germany, who handles jewelry made by great masters such as Braque, Ernst, Arp, and Picasso. Meeting GianCarlo Montebello, artist and jeweler, brother-in-law of the Pomodoro brothers, friend of Man Ray, of Soto, Niki de Saint Phalle, Meret Oppenheim, and of so many other artists with whom he has collaborated, working indefatigably for the recognition of this art form, encouraged me greatly.

And I wouldn't like to forget Marina Filippini in Verona, Chus Burés in Madrid, Sara Benda in New York, or Elisabetta Cipriani in London.

For some years now I have been drawn further into this world, and have called on various artists for a contribution. In certain cases, my request corresponded to the fundamentals of their working methods, as with César, to whom I gave chain bracelets and pendants from my family which he then compressed, or with Chamberlain, who out of friendship offered me his first-ever piece of jewelry, a painted and crumpled piece of aluminum, mounted as a brooch. Other artists also agreed to follow their example: Orlan, Wim Delvoye, Jacques Villeglé, Jean-Jacques Lebel, and Arne Quinze. Often, the artists started off by declining the order and the particular constraints of the job. Then in the intimacy of their studio, they were tempted to put their artistic vocabulary to the test of the change of scale. And so it was that Frank Stella, after numerous refusals, arrived one day with a package under his arm containing a necklace, a design made of titanium, crudely painted gold. The story of this collection is thus largely that of my friendships. It is also the fruit of many journeys undertaken to track down rare pieces. It is indeed frequent that the trace of artists' jewelry is lost. In which case I lead an investigation, from encounter to encounter.

Certain people, such as Joan Sonnabend from Boston, remember wonderful evenings during the course of which the women adorned themselves with their Man Ray or with their Fontana jewelry. Her very precious memories put me on the trail of various pieces. In some cases, my research went backward: having found a piece of jewelry at a dealer, I had to try to reconstitute its history. So it was that Germana Matta was inspired to tell me how Matta literally arranged a piece of jewelry himself, around her neck, or around her finger, or that my Greek friend Maria Demetriades recognized a necklace by Takis which had been molded on her body thirty years previously. These anecdotes show the specificity of these objects which combine both a personal history and the history of art. The border between them is subtle, and the wife of an artist knows all too well how porous it can be. I collect designs, aesthetically pleasing, of course, but also narratives of life. These works glitter with the love, the friendship, and the challenges that led to their creation. It didn't take more than that for my passion to be transformed into a collection, and it is now my turn to show these sculpted works of jewelry to the eyes of the public.

This book reflects all these passions. I hope that it represents a state of mind and mean it in no way to be didactic. Rather than organizing the pieces by alphabetical order or by category, I chose simply to follow my heart. My gratitude goes naturally to the professionals of the museums who put their confidence in me, to Sylvette and Bruno Gaudichon who were the first people to offer me the chance to show these collections at La Piscine of Roubaix and thanks to them, today at the Museum of Art and Design in New York, whose enthusiastic team around Holly Hotchner and Dorothy Globus collaborated with me to present an even more ambitious show to an American and international public.

Front row: Henri de La Celle,
Niki de Saint-Phalle, François-Xavier Lalanne;
back row: Annie de La Celle,
Jean Tinguely, and Claude Lalanne, c. 1959

Art as Jewelry

BY BARBARA ROSE

There has traditionally existed a marked distinction between art and craft. Painting and sculpture belonged to the first category, jewelry to the latter. Very few fine artists made jewelry before the modern period. Among the exceptions was the Florentine Renaissance sculptor, Benvenuto Cellini, whose patrons gave him stones which Cellini then set in elaborate baubles of precious metal. Few jewelers were considered original artists as well as artisans. Peter Karl Fabergé, who turned jewelry into an art form, was not a painter or sculptor, although his elaborate creations made him easily as famous as his artist contemporaries. Wealthy nobles of Russia kept their riches in the form of jewels which from time to time they gave to Fabergé to set in exquisite miniatures made in the style of decorated Easter eggs using precious metals and gemstones rather than more mundane materials.

In the late eighteenth century, Romanticism had a profound impact on the development of western jewelry, and mourning jewelry in the form of jet brooches became popular. In France Napoleon revived high style and introduced *parures*, suites of matching jewelry, such as the matching diamond-encrusted tiaras, earrings, rings, brooches, and necklaces which were designed for both of Napoleon's wives. In the United States, Charles Lewis Tiffany founded a modern production studio that produced precious jewelry for a broader clientele, pieces that were not unique or dominated by individual craftsman and aristocratic patronage.

Around 1900 the various craft movements propelled individual handmade artisanship into the spotlight once again. Jewelers began to explore the potential of the growing art nouveau style and the closely related German Jugendstil, the British and American Arts and Crafts Movement, Catalan Modernisme, Austro-Hungarian Sezession, and Italian "Liberty." Today these pieces can be seen in design and decorative arts museums but the names of their creators are rarely remembered. On the other hand, René Lalique, working for the Paris shop of Samuel Bing, was recognized by contemporaries as a leading figure with a personal style. Many date the history of modern art jewelry to Lalique and the decorative artists of the Arts and Crafts and art nouveau movements. Their relief techniques were closely related to sculptural carving; the American sculptor Augustus Saint-Gaudens learned to carve working for French stone cameo cutters in New York. The overlap between sculpture and hand-crafted individual pieces of jewelry may really be said to begin with Catalan Modernisme, a style that covered all media including architecture. Among its most famous practitioners were architect Antoni Gaudí who did indeed design jewelry and sculptor Julio González, whose activity as a jewelry designer paralleled his career as the first sculptor to work with forged iron. Using a similar technique of soldering metal parts together, González created extraordinary rings, pins, bracelets, and necklaces. His strong and bold works suggested the possibility that artists could make body ornaments that were like miniature artworks.

In Germany the Bauhaus taste for simplified forms and modern materials such as plastics and aluminum widened the range of materials artists could use to produce jewelry. Crafts at the Bauhaus were given almost equal weight for the first time as the major arts and thus the line between them was effaced to the point that painters, sculptors, and architects felt comfortable making artisanal objects. Textile artist Anni Albers led the way in working with found materials, producing pieces in direct contrast to the opulence and ostentation of traditional jewelry. The Bauhaus-trained Albers made a 1941 brooch from an aluminum sink strainer from which paper clips were suspended. These influenced students of Josef Albers like Robert Rauschenberg to use junk to create sculptures.

In Paris famous artists such as Picasso and Man Ray brought new respect to jewelry as an art form. They designed works for goldsmiths to produce but the finished pieces still bear the mark of the artists—whether Braque, Derain, or Dalí—who designed them. The hand of the artisan became an extension of that of the artist who was not a skilled metalsmith. Sculptor Alexander Calder was able to translate his sculptural style directly.

The most prolific of the great artists who designed jewelry, Calder personally produced 1,800 different pieces. Calder was inspired by African cultures, the exotic, and the avant-garde when he lived in Paris in the 1920s. His jewelry reflects his many different interests. Calder was the first artist to make jewelry a successful form of modern sculpture. Some were forms of the friends' initials, as for example the spiral of silver initials *O.K.*, a gift to Georgia O'Keeffe that she regularly wore to

THE HAND OF THE ARTISAN BECAME AN EXTENSION OF THAT OF THE ARTIST WHO WAS NOT A SKILLED METALSMITH.

fasten the kimono dresses that became her uniform. Calder also designed mobile pieces that were set in motion by the wearer's body, thus launching the mode for jewelry by sculptors that resembled miniatures of their three-dimensional works.

Although Calder made all his own pieces using the techniques of his wire sculptures, many artists entrusted the realization of their designs to Milan's Gem Montebello studio. Gem Montebello produced designs by Man Ray, and had a reputation for turning out some of the most fascinating and imaginative artist-made jewelry during this period. GianCarlo Montebello founded this workshop in 1967 in order to collaborate with artists of international reputation. Many of the world's most famous artists had their designs in precious metals and stones realized there. For example,

Belgian sculptor Pol Bury created his kinetic jewelry in collaboration with Gem Montebello. Man Ray was particularly interested in jewelry because beside being a surrealist painter and object maker he was also a skilled fashion photographer. Most of his jewels were made in the early 1970s but their designs are based on earlier drawings and sculptures.

Today, painters and sculptors make jewelry as tokens of affection for loved ones to be worn as the medieval knight carried a token of his lady love. Not surprisingly sculptors are frequently the most successful jewelry designers because they are already working in three dimensions. Often their jewels frequently resemble miniatures of their monumental works. The jewelry of contemporary artists, Anthony Caro, Giò and Arnaldo Pomodoro, and Niki de Saint Phalle and Bernar Venet is closely related to their sculptural styles. Jewels by fine artists are recognizable because they are a translation into wearable objects of their own personal styles. Thus pop artists like Roy Lichtenstein, Op artists like Vasarely, and color field painters like Jack Youngerman designed wearable multiples to be made in limited editions. The individuality and surprise of jewelry by artists makes it especially intriguing to collectors, who are often friends of the artists. The sentiments of these collectors are summed up by Peggy Guggenheim, a collector of Calder's jewelry, in her autobiography: "I am the only woman in the world who wears his enormous mobile earrings." Given Calder's prodigious output this was not entirely true, but it neatly encapsulatess the pride of the wearer of jewelry by a famous artist.

Above and following pages: Jean-Auguste-Dominique Ingres, *Madame Moitessier*, (details), 1851, oil on canvas, 147 x 100 cm, Washington, National Gallery of Art.

DIANE'
JEWELS

S The ancient goddess Diana is a goddess without jewels. She leaves them to Juno, to Venus, or to that insignificant, frivolous mortal who goes by the name of "Psyche"—not that she has much psychology to speak of.

Hence innumerable paintings entitled *Psyche Showing Her Sisters the Jewels She Received from Cupid*. Enough said. Occasionally statues of Diana display a crescent moon on the forehead, something Diane de Poitiers was to recall on the banks of the River Loire. In Rome though Diana's real jewels are her bow and the arrows in her quiver. Instruments made of metal, full of strength, simple in form: the tools of the huntress. When Bernar Vernet is asked if he designs bows because they are Diana's symbol—his wife's symbol—he bursts into laughter and does not answer. As a girl Diane Venet remembers being given engravings, and even a small painting, depicting Diana the Huntress. They can still be found today in their studio-home in Muy, as guestroom decorations. She has forgotten that it may be the origin, if not of Bernar's sculptures, at least of a shrewd trait of her character. Now she has become a huntress herself, a collector. The people who gave her those prints must have seen that already as a child she loved art, sensing perhaps that the creative impulse would form the very center of her life.

At those endless arty dinners in Venice, Basel, and Miami, during which she never looks bored, art world viragos vie with one another with their malevolently shimmering diamonds and rubies, sapphires, and emeralds. Diane sports instead a single piece of jewelry on which she is complimented in an undertone by some friend in the know—gallery-owner, museum curator, or historian of twentieth-century art.

BUT DIANE DOES NOT LOVE HERSELF IN THEM. SHE LOV INTO WHICH SHE BREATHES

She has put Diderot's *Les bijoux indiscrets* back on the library shelf and now defends and promotes more "discreet" jewels. Her wide ranging interests, however, come more from Diderot's *Encyclopedia*. The jewelry by contemporary artists she possesses today forms a unique reference collection. Like a *Who's Who* of modern artists, the catalog of her pieces here retells the history of twentieth-century art. It is as if she had the Musée National d'Art Moderne in the Centre Pompidou, or MOMA, slung around her neck.... While, as photographs show, that great collector and "huntress-down" of jewels Peggy Guggenheim would hang hers like paintings from a rail above her bed, Diane prefers to arrange them in boxes (not jewel-cases), or, more importantly, to take them out and wear them so as to instill life into them. It is by displaying her jewelry on her body that Diane Venet flies the flag for those she admires and fights for the artists she loves.

But Diane does not love jewels simply because she can

JEWELS BECAUSE SHE CAN DRAPE
ES THEM AS SHE WOULD A SCULPTURE
LIFE, WHICH TELLS HER A STORY.

drape herself in them. She loves them as she would a sculpture into which she breathes life, one which tells a story—often one she appears in, or at least that she witnessed. Opening one of her boxes at home she speaks of her enduring love of art. On the evening of the dinner held in the Orangery of the Château of Versailles to mark the opening of the 2011 exhibition Venet à Versailles, she wore a single piece, a necklace, just as she always does at Bernar's private views—a work by "her" artist.

Diane the jewelry collector thus steers clear of gemsetters and the Place Vendôme. She understands how, if Benvenuto Cellini, whom she often mentions, carved his *Perseus* on the Piazza della Signoria in Florence with all the skill of a goldsmith, he considered his jewels as sculpture and his abiding ambition was to outdo Michelangelo. However talented they may be, the artists brought together by Diane are not jewelers as such: they are artists who make jewels.

Pride of place in Diane's collection goes all to the gifts she has received from friends, frequently presents from Bernar Venet. There's a ring by Arman; and a 1970 pendant incorporating a watch. Very recently, Jacques Villeglé designed a ring for her. One of her fondest memories is the day Frank Stella—who for years looked quizzical when she dared mention jewelry and who never really pictured himself as a silversmith—arrived bearing a package containing a necklace. Perhaps this was the day Diane's jewelry collection earned its legendary status.

Since then she has commissioned a great deal and artists have presented her with many jewels. It is true that they tend to turn their hand to jewelry as gifts for those closest to them: Sol LeWitt created rings for his daughters; Takis started with one-offs. Jean-Jacques Lebel made Diane a necklace out of rifle bullets unearthed in flea markets and tiny, low-value coins. When she wears it she looks at once like an ironic Danae drenched in pennies and a parodic victim "rained on" with "lead." It has echoes of Ingres who, as he embarked on the portrait of Madame Moitessier in a black dress, chose from one of his model's jewel-cases a bracelet decorated with coins to give her the air of

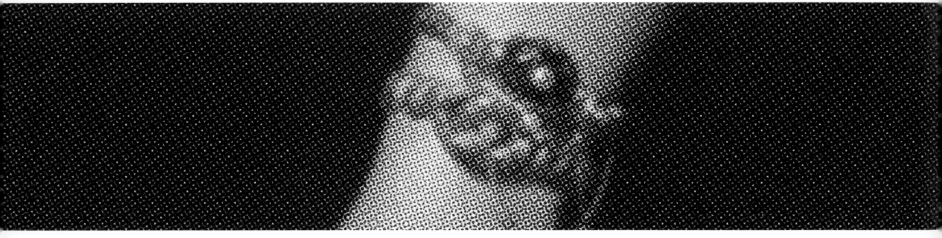

DIANA'S REAL JEWELS ARE HER BOW AND TH
IN HER QUIVER. INSTRUMENTS MADE OF MET
SIMPLE IN FORM: THE TOOLS OF THE HUNTR

an ancient goddess. Among the "grapeshot," of Lebel's piece one catches sight of the profile of Lincoln or of Queen Elizabeth II or the symbol that signaled the advent of the euro. A recent arrival in Diane's collection, it is a necklace that affords her especial delight. Diane recalls purchasing an enamel brooch from Roy Lichtenstein in New York in 1967. First and foremost a souvenir of the many happy hours she had spent in front of his works, it was a modest item and could hardly be termed a jewel. Yet, issued in what was probably quite a large edition at the time, it has today become extremely scarce, almost unobtainable. At the end of a private view for one of his shows Robert Rauschenberg gave Diane a brooch she'd liked with a little red truck on it. She was not yet a collector, but she has kept it with her like a talisman. Once again it is the story behind the piece—a peep into the art world—that renders it so unique.

Some artists stumble into jewelry by sheer chance: Elsa Schiaparelli handed Giacometti a commission for buttons to go on her gowns. Inevitably they were too heavy, so Giacometti turned them into brooches that he pre-sented as gifts—and the sculptures became jewels. Other artists make editions of their jewelry. When Diane wears Picasso's *Little Faun* as a pendant on a gold chain, she explains how it was made in Aix, in the workshop of François Hugo, who also produced small sculptures by Dorothea Tanning, Cocteau, and Max Ernst. These are for the most part limited editions—as with the jewels by Braque that Heger De Loewenfeld realized while the artist was still alive. When Diane Venet wears a *LOVE* ring by Robert Indiana, it is such a signature piece, rehashed in posters, magazines, and postcards, that one might be forgiven for thinking it's a museum spin-off. In fact, it is one of the very rare gold versions of the ring, an edition of which the artist gifted to his companion.

Certain artists like to be immediately identifiable: Anish Kapoor's rings are miniature works by Anish Kapoor. Pol Bury has produced replicas of his sculptures scaled down into jewelry, though Diane prefers a 1970s bracelet that moves when she wears it, making a dull jangle that only she can hear above the hum of conversation. It's only when she has the piece on that it comes to life as a sculpture. And, when she wears the bracelet, it instantly transforms her into part of a work of art.

Diane is still collecting today, still scouring the horizon for pieces of historical value. Occasionally she catches sight of something jealously guarded by a society woman famous in the 1960s. But why then doesn't she possess anything by Line Vautrin? She has nothing against her work, but Vautrin is exclusively a creator

ARROWS

AL, FULL OF STRENGTH,

ESS.

SHE WAS NOT YET A COLLECTOR, BUT SHE
LIKE A TALISMAN. ONCE AGAIN IT IS THE
PEEP INTO THE ART WORLD—THAT RENDERS

of jewels, and Diane only goes in for works by sculptors and painters. Because Diane possesses all the rigor and discernment typical of the true collector. Her collection covers several periods in the history of artists' jewelry, beginning with the postwar era, with Giacometti and Picasso, quickly followed by a second phase focusing on those great makers who turned to artists for their designs. The whole history of art in the south of France at the time, centered on Montebello and Hugo, flashes before our eyes. There are also—unexpected perhaps in such a collection, but a notable strong point nonetheless—jewels by American artists who on the face of it one might think unlikely to bother with personal adornment. This is perhaps because, according to the exacting criteria of Diane Venet, jewelry has precious little to do with "appearances." And Diane's contention that jewelry should be regarded as art—an art halfway between sculpture and installation—is a genuine art historical idea. These pieces of twentieth- and early twenty-first-century jewelry demonstrate that it can no longer be dis-

missed as a minor or decorative art. A jewel can be a fully fledged artwork, as in the Renaissance Cellini had already tried to convince his contemporaries, arguing against Giorgio Vasari who was determined to relegate him to the level of a master craftsman. One can be sure that no-one knows the jewelry holdings of the Musée des Arts Décoratifs in Paris and those of the Victoria & Albert Museum in London better than Diane.

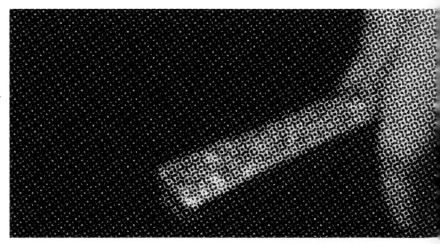

HAS KEPT IT WITH HER

STORY BEHIND THE PIECE—A

T SO UNIQUE.

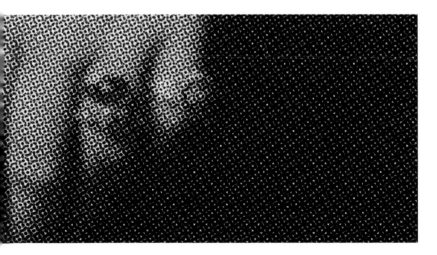

She first showed a selection from her own collection in Roubaix (a town in a region of northern France where her family has its roots), in a splendid museum called La Piscine (the swimming pool), but for all that she does not think of her jewels as museum pieces.

Nothing will stop Diane's collection growing further, especially now she is increasingly turning to emerging talents on the art scene. From Kader Attia she ordered some two-fingered "shackles" that have already become famous. She displays an interest too in YBAs (Young British Artists).

Finally, Diane the huntress is a feminist—in any case she is convinced of the equality of men and women when it comes to jewelry. Dorothea Tanning, Brigitte Nahon, Pierrette Bloch: these are the names of some of the female artists who have made jewelry, and to whom Diane affords a place of honor. She has also recently presented Bernar Venet with a gold mask made by Man Ray inspired by driving goggles. If the dozens of little holes bored in the face don't let in the wind, they certainly give the wearer's eyes a different look. Housed in its box, it glows like the visage of a Mycenaean king.

It has to be confessed that artists have not overexerted themselves in jewelry for men—if one excludes Claude Lalanne's cufflinks that entered the annals of literary posterity when one was gobbled up by Bernard Frank's washing machine… Indeed, male jewelry remains uncharted territory. But Diane is waiting; she has presents to give. It just needs artists to be more inventive.

Avant-gardes

Grande Tête ronde, 1952
Pendant
Gold, diameter: 2⅜ in. (6 cm)
1/8, edition François Hugo
Diane Venet collection

28

André Derain

Chatou 1880–Garches 1954

Fascinated by antiquity and literature, the young André Derain spent a lot of time at the Louvre, where he used to make copies of ancient works. He met Henri Matisse there, and later Maurice de Vlaminck, and all three became founders of the Fauvist movement in 1905. But the character of Derain was complex, and his style evolved with him. His work was alternately influenced by cubism and African art, before he turned to more muted colors and returned to a more "academic" production.

In the 1940s he created the wax models for his jewelry *Faune*, *Crétoise*, and *Masque*, jewelry which he made as a present for his wife. He entrusted its production to his friend, the goldsmith François Hugo, at whose marriage he had been witness. All in all, ten pendants and brooches were made in twenty-three-carat gold, then hand-hammered in a steel die. Each model (they were each produced in an edition of six) was slightly different as a result of this technique. They are geometrical heads with jagged edges, characteristic of the double influence of cubism and archaeology in the artist's work. Derain then turned to making "portable sculptures." Recuperating the lead from his tubes of paint, he molded it into the shape of lips, the St. Andrew's cross, and even a pair of buttocks.

Faune, 1950s, pendant, 23-carat gold, diameter: 3¾ in. (9.5 cm)
2/6, edition François Hugo
Didier Antiques collection

29

Georges Braque
Argenteuil 1882–Paris 1963

When Georges Braque declared in 1961: "It is not enough to show what is painted, you still need to touch it," he was already the creator of a colossal output of paintings. Inspired by the Fauvist painters Matisse and Derain, whom he discovered at the Salon d'Automne in Paris in 1905, and impressed by the approach to volume in paintings by Cézanne, he collaborated with Picasso whom he met at the Bateau Lavoir in 1906. In 1909 Braque finished his *Grand Nu*: cubism was born. At almost eighty years of age, in the final two years of his life, he realized he had not produced many three-dimensional works. To remedy this, he asked to be introduced to Baron Heger de Loewenfeld. His collaboration with the famous jeweler whom he nicknamed "the continuation of my hand" was a triumph. The period of his *Métamorphoses* was in full swing. The creations were inspired by Greek mythology, especially the metaphysical theme of flight, and the interpretation of Hesiod's *Theogony*. This attraction for antiquity combined with his desire to create objects to inspire his jewelry named after Greek heroes. Braque supplied preparatory drawings in the form of gouache, and Heger de Loewenfeld carefully crafted the jewelry using the most noble of materials. All in all, more than 110 gouaches ended up as jewelry.

His success was crowned in May 1963, when André Malraux organized the first exhibition of Jewelry by Braque at the Louvre. Malraux declared on seeing the work: "This is Braque's masterpiece." After this, more than two hundred exhibitions worldwide were dedicated to him. On the death of Baron Heger de Lowenfeld, Armand Israël, curator of the Braque museum in Saint-Dié-des-Vosges, brought out a new collection of jewelry in editions of eight inscribed "Bijoux de Braque." This production is different from the one made during Braque's lifetime that consisted of editions of seventy-five, signed collectively by Braque and Heger de Loewenfeld.

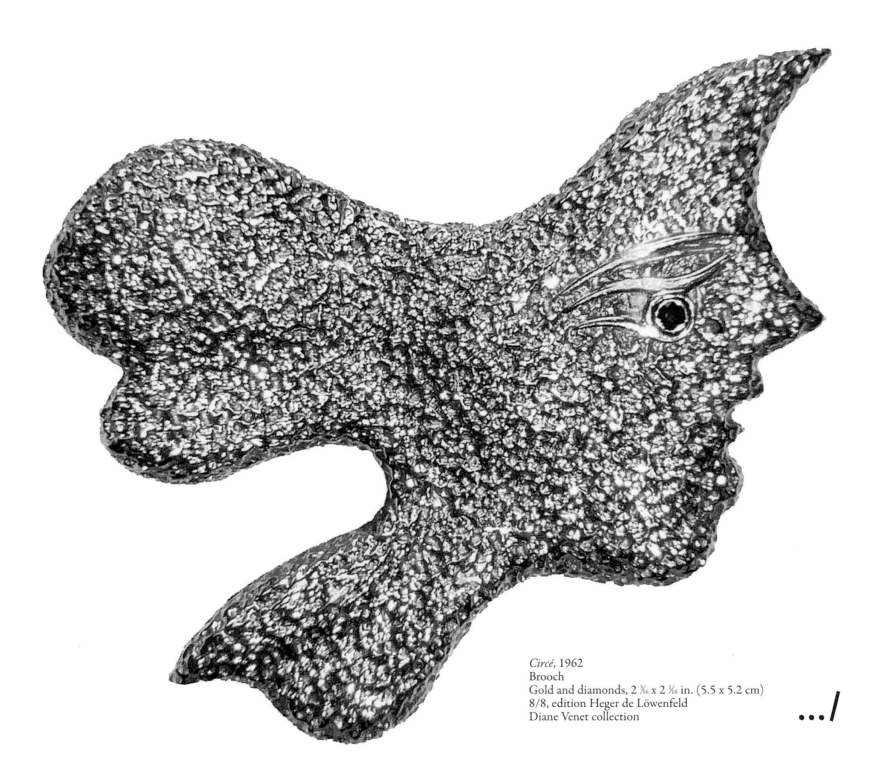

Circé, 1962
Brooch
Gold and diamonds, 2 ³⁄₁₆ x 2 ¹⁄₁₆ in. (5.5 x 5.2 cm)
8/8, edition Heger de Löwenfeld
Diane Venet collection

.../

Oiseau Térée, 1963
Brooch, 18-carat gold and rubies,
2 ³⁄₁₆ x 2 ¹⁄₁₆ in. (5.5 x 5.2 cm)
Unique, edition Heger de Löwenfeld
Diana Küppers collection

Trois Oiseaux les fils d'Eos, c. 1960
Brooch, three different golds,
1³⁄₁₆ x 3¹⁄₈ in. (3 x 8 cm)
3/75, edition Heger de Löwenfeld
Diana Küppers collection

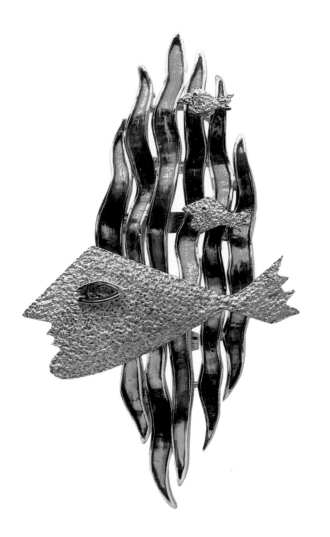

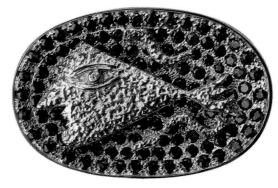

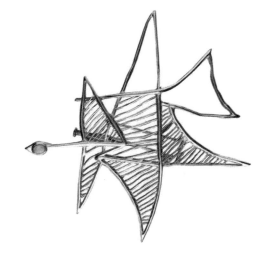

Hero, 1962
Brooch, Gold, sapphire, and diamond,
1¼ x 2⅟₁₆ in. (3.3 x 5.2 cm)
1/8, edition Heger de Löwenfeld
Diana Küppers collection

Hera, c. 1960
Brooch, Gold, sapphire, and diamond eye,
1¼ x 1 ¹³⁄₁₆ in. (3.2 x 4.8 cm)
1/8, edition Heger de Löwenfeld
Diane Venet collection

Asteria, 1963
Brooch, 18-carat gold and emerald eye,
3 ⁷⁄₁₆ x 2¹³⁄₁₆ in. (8.7 x 7.2 cm)
Edition Heger de Löwenfeld
Diane Venet collection

Pablo Picasso

Málaga 1881—Mougins 1973

Celebrated for his cubist paintings, Picasso was the most eclectic of artists, using countless different media and materials in his works. In the mid-1950s, he made several necklaces from small shells for his partner Dora Maar. His production of gold jewelry began in 1956 in Aix-en-Provence. He was trying to find someone who could make a silver version of a platter he had created in white ceramic. His terra-cotta platters of this period were realized by the pottery workshop Madoura in Vallauris, but Picasso was troubled by the fragility of clay. Having long been passionate about the work of Renaissance goldsmiths, he wanted to resurrect their centuries-old traditions, and to confer on his dishes the hardness of metal. Finding the right person to execute such a technical feat was no easy matter, however, especially as he was dead set against having his designs cast. It was his friend, the critic Douglas Cooper, who found a solution, suggesting a collaboration with the goldsmith François Hugo. The great-grandson of the poet executed a platter in silver repoussé named *The Sleeper*: it was realized completely by hand without casting of any kind. Picasso was delighted with the result, and it marked the beginning of a long collaboration and a lasting friendship.

It was through the solving of another technical problem that their association evolved toward the elaboration of jewelry. In 1960, the creation of a large compote dish decorated with three mythological figures turned out badly. They decided to separate the bacchante, the pipe player, and the cymbals player and to shape them all in gold. It was the beginning of the production of medallions. François Hugo made a series of twenty-three-carat gold medallions that closely echoed Picasso's drawings and ceramic models. We find the same recurring themes as in the work of the master: bull-fighting, fauna, faces, fish....

A surprising fact marked the creation of these objects made with the goldsmith: Picasso kept every one of them as if they were treasures. He refused to even exhibit them or to issue them in larger numbers. It was not until 1967 that a limited mass production, intended for sale, appeared.

Le Grand Faune, 1973
After Pablo Picasso
Brooch
23-carat gold, 3¼ x 4¾ in.
(8.5 x 12 cm)
20/20, edition François Hugo
Diane Venet collection

...∕

.../Pablo Picasso

Poisson, After Pablo Picasso, 1973, Brooch, 23-carat gold, 1¾ x 1¹⁵⁄₁₆ in. (4.4 x 5 cm), 18/20, edition François Hugo, Diane Venet collection

Visage rond, After Pablo Picasso, 1972, Brooch, 23-carat gold, diameter: 1¹⁵⁄₁₆ (5 cm), 16/20, edition François Hugo, Diane Venet collection

Médaillon oval, After Pablo Picasso, 1972, Brooch, 23-carat gold, 1 ⅜ x 2 ¹⁄₁₆ in. (3.5 x 5.3 cm) 5/20, edition François Hugo, Diane Venet collection

Trèfle, After Pablo Picasso, 1972, Brooch, Gold, 1¾ x 2⅛ (4.4 x 5.4 cm) 9/20, edition François Hugo, Diane Venet collection

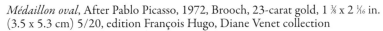

...

Facing page: Pablo Picasso, *Portrait de Dora Maar de profil*, Boisgeloup, March 1936 Photograph, 9½ x 7¼ in. (24 x 18.2 cm), Paris, Musée Picasso, Picasso archives

Visage aux taches,
After Pablo Picasso, 1972
Brooch
Gold, diameter: 1⅞ in. (5 cm)
4/20, edition François Hugo
Diane Venet collection

Facing page: *Tête*, 1950, pendant, silver, diameter: 1⅜ in. (3.5 cm)
Unique, Naïla de Monbrison collection

Alexander Calder

Lawnton, Pennsylvania 1898–New York 1976

The American artist Alexander Calder was a prolific maker of jewelry. His output of almost 1,800 pieces is characterized by recurring spiral shapes that symbolize eternity, and the use of copper, brass, gilded bronze, and occasionally silver. Two exhibitions at the Willard Gallery in New York in 1940 and 1941 exhibited his jewelry, without much commercial success. From 1926 onward, after he had produced *Calder's Circus*, a sculpture made of wire figurines, Calder took to working with these easily moldable metals. After installing the *Circus* in Paris, Calder abandoned figurative representation and, influenced by Piet Mondrian, worked on abstract compositions that developed into "mobiles" in 1930, then "stabiles" in 1960.

At the age of eight, the child prodigy was already making trinkets for his sister Peggy's dolls. Throughout his life he designed and constructed items of jewelry as gifts for his close family and friends, particularly for his wife Louisa. His creations are all unique pieces. Most of the jewelry Calder produced was impulsive: he didn't think about composition, instead letting the shape evolve with wire in his hands or with a hammer.

Untitled, undated
Belt buckle / Pendant
Gilded bronze
Diameter 4⅝ in. (11.7 x 11.4 cm)
Unique
Diane Venet collection

Untitled, 1945, Cuff bracelets
Brass wire, 5 x 2⅝ x 2¼ in. and 5¼ x 2¾ x 2¼ in.
(12.7 x 6.6 x 5.7 cm and 13.3 x 7 x 5.7 cm)
Unique, Patricia Pastor Friedman collection

...l

41

.../ Alexander Calder

Untitled, 1935
Necklace
Brass wire and cord, 14½ in. (36.8 cm)
Unique
Patricia Pastor Friedman collection

.../

Facing page: Man Ray, *Louisa Calder*, Castagna Calder series, photograph,
Musée National d'Art Moderne, Centre Pompidou, Paris

43

Untitled, 1935
Bracelet
Brass wire and cord, 2¼ x 3½ in.(4.4 x 8.9 cm)
Unique
Patricia Pastor Friedman collection

Untitled, 1939
Necklace
Gilded bronze, diameter: 16½ in. (42 cm)
Unique
Louisa Guinness collection

45

Harry Bertoia

San Lorenzo 1915–Pennsylvania 1978

Metalwork was predominant in Harry Bertoia's work. During his studies in the United States, this Italian-born artist learned the techniques of design and working with metal. Indeed design was his first interest, and he collaborated for many years with both the Knoll and the Eames couples, whom he had met during his training. In 1952, while working for Knoll, he invented his famous Diamond Chair, an iconic model in which the all-encompassing air glides into spaces left vacant in a molded lattice work of welded steel. The chair became such a success that Harry Bertoia was free to dedicate himself to his sculpture. He turned his talents toward working with metal that he stretched or bent and manipulated to produce sound.

During World War II, the shortage of materials prevented him from working on larger works in his workshop. He decided to dedicate himself to creating jewelry, mostly wedding bands. Throughout his life, he made jewelry for his friends and family in silver and gold, and exhibited many times with Alexander Calder. His later jewelry used curved lines, and was created in different materials such as brass, iron, and even hand-tooled bronze. Spirals, crosses, and cubes are recurring shapes in his work. The empty spaces, letting the air pass through, play a role as important as the meticulous working of the metal.

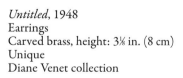

Untitled, 1948
Earrings
Carved brass, height: 3⅛ in. (8 cm)
Unique
Diane Venet collection

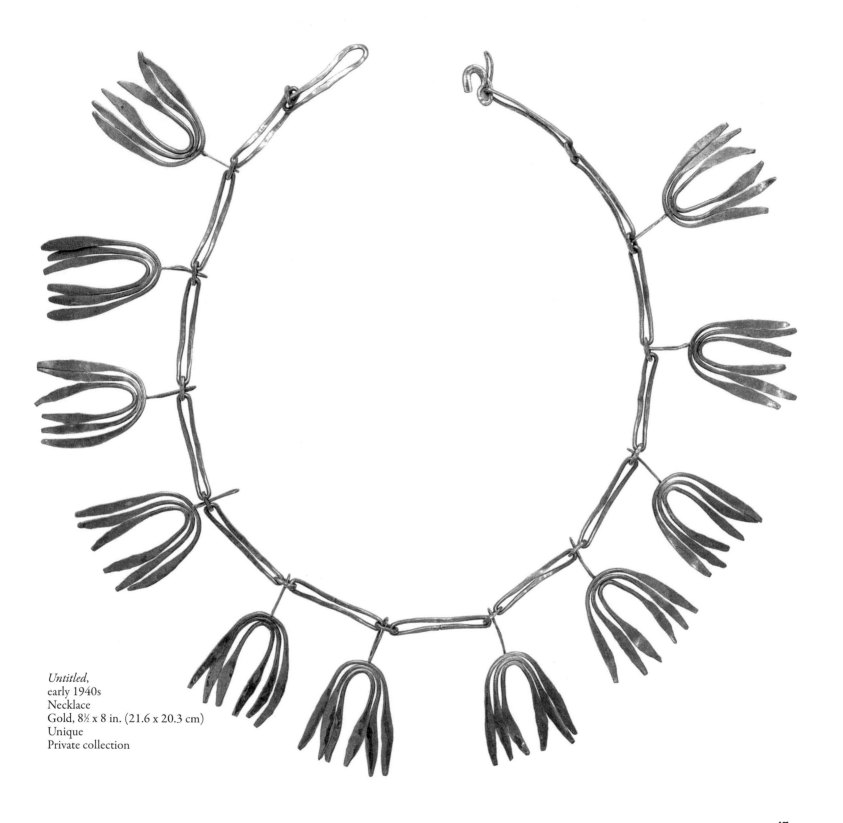

Untitled,
early 1940s
Necklace
Gold, 8½ x 8 in. (21.6 x 20.3 cm)
Unique
Private collection

Gino Severini

Cortona 1883–Paris 1966

Gino Severini decomposed movement and light with his cubo-futuristic approach to painting. Close to Giacomo Balla and Umberto Boccioni, on February 11, 1910 he became a signatory to the Manifesto of Futurist Painting. Severini supported the ideas of futurism, and contributed to the movement with an almost scientific approach, but in a style all of his own. Having settled in Paris in 1906, he discovered the works of Seurat as well as cubism, both of which would have a big influence on his painting. At that time, his compositions were marked by themes of cabarets and dancers, as shown in his 1911 canvas *The Haunting Dancer*. From 1924, Severini experimented with the techniques of mosaic and the mural, decorating palaces and churches with monumental frescoes. Whatever the media, he enjoyed spending time on works brimming with rhythm and populated with memories.

In the 1940s, he copied some of his models into gold and silver, and created a bracelet, a one-off piece reminiscent of a slave bracelet. In 1960, he designed a deconstructed brooch, similar to the synthetic cubism of his paintings. He confided the preparatory drawings, realized in tempera, to the Roman jewelers Masenza, asking them to produce the *Spilla* in gold and stones of different colors.

Untitled, 1940s
Bangle
Silver and gold, height: 1⅝ in. (4.1 cm),
diameter: 2⅞ in. (7.3 cm)
Unique
Diane Venet collection

Pequeña star, 1990
Brooch, adapted from an original sculpture of 1925
Silver, 2¾ x 3 x 1¼ in. (7 x 8 x 3 cm)
4/7, edition Atelier Pierrette Gargallo
Private collection

Pablo Gargallo

Maella 1881–Reus 1934

Pablo Gargallo's sculptures are characterized by his knowledge of metalwork and forging technique—his father was a blacksmith. His first creations in brass sheets and wires soon led on to monumental sculptures in iron, in which the analytical decomposition of light and shade play a dominating role. The artist used figures of harlequins, Kiki de Montparnasse, and other naked women as his principal tools of expression. An artist whose style sits between modernity and tradition, Pablo Gargallo removed the decorative connotations from metal, and as such was the precursor of artists such as González and David Smith.

His jewelry output can be divided into two distinct categories. The first group came about due to a lung disease from which he suffered between 1915 and 1916 that forced the artist to concentrate on creating small-scale works. His themes were masks, fauna, and women, all previously used in his sculpture. At the same time, he exhibited a series of jewelry at a prestigious jewelry store in the Passeig de Gracia in Barcelona, where he incorporated a formal approach into the traditional elements of the jewelry, using precious stones and traditional work with gold.

The second series, which Gargallo undertook from 1925, was based on three-dimensional heads which he used as preparatory studies for his large-format sculptures. Thus the silver brooch *Pequeña Star* of 1925 became the model for the sculpture of the same name in 1927. The mindful attention Gargallo paid to volume in his jewelry work permitted him to test new techniques and a new iconography.

49

Henri Étienne-Martin Loriol 1913–Paris 1995

After studying at the École des Beaux Arts in Lyon and membership of the Lyonnais group Témoignage, Henri Étienne-Martin settled in Paris where he discovered the art of Marcel Duchamp, the surrealists, and abstraction, which marked him profoundly. One of his most striking works was an eight-meter high virgin sculpted out of soft rock that was intentionally left in its natural outdoor environment to deteriorate, during World War II. Toward the end of the 1940s he established his real artistic vocabulary, populated with solid elements and those in relief, hollows sculpted in wood, plaster, or bronze. He was imbued with a deep spirituality and interested in Eastern religions, and borrowed various forms from the ancient Orient. In 1954 he began the series known as the *Demeures* (Dwellings), comprised of a sort of cavernous architecture which made reference to his childhood and to the house where he lived at that time. He declared about it: "This house is me, with all my contradictions, and the rooms are the paths of my thoughts."

The brooch-pendant *Médaille petite demeure* (Medal of a Small Dwelling) is an integral part of this series. Produced in gold by the editors Artcurial in 1988 in an edition of twenty-five, it shows the same sinuous lines as those made on a much bigger scale. Close to the aesthetics of Gaudí, Henri Étienne-Martin is also the author of anthropomorphic sculptures which echo forms taken from the plant world.

Médaille petite demeure, 1988
Pendant
Gold, 1¾ x 1⅞ x ¾ in.
(4.5 x 4.8 x 1.8 cm)
3/25, edition Artcurial
Nicole Galibert collection

Giacomo Balla
Turin 1871–Rome 1958

Movement, light, and color are the elements that form the core of the work of Giacomo Balla. Founder member of futurism in 1910 with Filippo Marinetti and Umberto Boccioni, he developed an art inspired by the machine, and in particular the speed of automobiles. In 1912, he presented a work that would become symbolic, *Dynamism of a Dog on a Leash*, which deconstructed the movements of a dog's legs using repetitive sequences and touches of color. He then devoted himself to sculpture and modeled *Boccioni's Fist* in 1914. After World War I, sullied by suspicions of having embraced fascist ideology, he detached himself from the futurists and continued his artistic exploits alone. Influenced by cubism, he leaned toward abstraction for a short while, then reverted to becoming a figurative artist in the 1930s. He turned to the cinema, then to design, creating several decorative objects in chrome-plated metal.

In 1992, Artcurial issued a posthumous series of his jewels, impressed by Balla's sensibility to movement in his drawings. Some of the gilded bronze enameled jewelry bears the names of his two daughters, Elica and Luce (helix and light), two major components of his body of work.

Elica Vermeil Brooch, 1992
Brooch
Gold plate and enamel, 2¹¹⁄₁₆ x 1¾ in.
(6.8 x 4.5 cm)
13/350, edition Artcurial
Diane Venet collection

Fernand Léger

Argentan 1888–Gif-sur-Yvette 1955

After his debuts as a draftsman in an architect's office, Fernand Léger set about becoming a painter alongside artists Sonia Delaunay, Alexandre Archipenko, and Jacques Lipchitz, whom he frequented at La Ruche, from 1908. In 1910, he was invited to exhibit in the gallery of the art dealer Daniel-Henry Kahnweiler, a fervent champion of Picasso and Braque. Fernand Léger, already inspired by the retrospective dedicated to Paul Cézanne in 1907, directed his exploration toward cubism. Having experienced war firsthand, he based his work on the mechanical motifs of machines, which become omnipresent in his oeuvre. Little by little, rhythm and color took a predominant place in his work. He pushed this research to its paroxysm in the Contrasts of Forms series of paintings in the early 1910s. The contrasts between the characters, the objects, and the abstract figures allow him, through his paintings, to express his idea of modernity as being the relationship between people. Influenced by the architect Le Corbusier, in the 1920s he created large-scale murals, then from 1937 mosaics and stained glass windows. Within the latter, he represented human beings in very simplistic compositions.

In the 1950s, he created a brooch in enameled metal, in an edition of one thousand copies. It was derived from the shapes and motifs of his paintings, with the predominant colors being yellow, red, blue, and green.

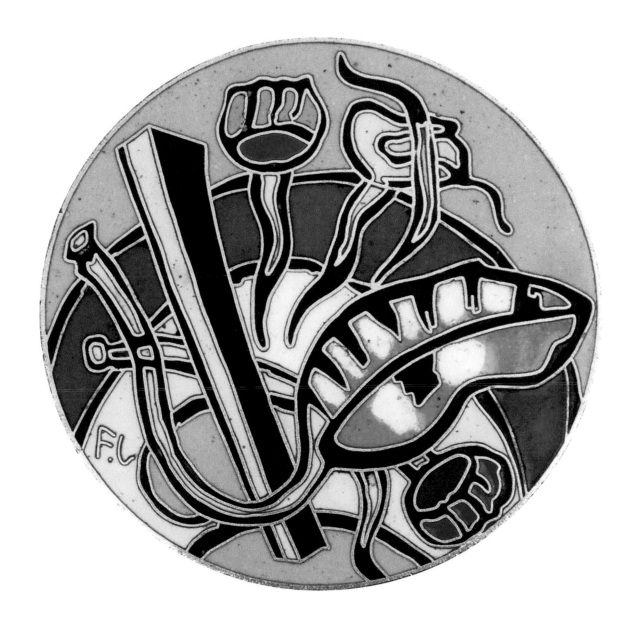

Untitled, 1950s
Brooch
Metal and enamel,
1⁹⁄₁₆ x 2³⁄₁₆ in. (4 x 5.5 cm)
165/1000
Diane Venet collection

Alberto Giacometti
Stampa 1901–Chur 1966

Encouraged by his father, Giovanni Giacometti, a respected post-Impressionist painter, Alberto Giacometti made his first drawings at the age of nine and his first sculpture when just fourteen. He then embarked on a study trip through Italy, taking inspiration from the monuments of the Classical period and the Renaissance in a range of paintings, sculptures, prints, and drawings.

At the beginning of the 1920s, he settled in Paris, where he became a pupil of the celebrated sculptor Antoine Bourdelle. There he also discovered Cubism, a pictorial approach he practiced from 1927 on. Thereafter he met many artists who were to prove an enduring influence, such as Constantin Brancusi, and then, in 1930, the head of Surrealism, André Breton. That same year he joined the Surrealist movement, before leaving it some five years later and reverting to a more rugged style of sculpture. His friendship with Jean-Paul Sartre and Simone de Beauvoir confirmed a predilection for works laden with symbolism and existentialism. After the War, during which he took refuge in Geneva, there first appeared the emaciated, elongated figures that characterize his oeuvre—among them, the famous *Man Walking* (1947). Naturally inclined to self-criticism, Alberto Giacometti was in the habit of destroying creations with which he was dissatisfied. In parallel with his solo output, in about 1935 he was also to collaborate with the interior designer Jean-Michel Frank, for whom he designed models for standard, bracket, and suspension lamps.

Around the same period, he was creating a line of jewelry for couturier Elsa Schiaparelli. Giacometti also made his mark in another series of jewels, for the most part brooches in patinated gilt bronze, silver or gold, with motifs derived from his artistic vocabulary and based on themes such as a man or a woman with raised arms, the propeller, the Angel of the Annunciation, the sphinx, or birds.

La Sirène, c. 1935
Brooch
Patinated bronze,
diameter: 1⅞ in. (4.7 cm)
Designed for Schiaparelli
Diane Venet collection

Untitled, c. 1935
Brooch
Patinated bronze,
diameter: 1⅞ in. (4.7 cm)
Elisabeth Royer collection

Arnaldo Pomodoro

Morciano di Romagna 1926–

Arnaldo Pomodoro experimented with metalwork in the 3P studio in Pescara, then opened a workshop in Milan with his brother Giò. In 1956, they both presented a selection of jewelry and sculpture at the Venice Biennale. This exhibition expanded their growing reputation and pushed them toward their individual artistic universes. Arnaldo moved toward creating sculpture populated with geometrical forms, through which he expressed his interest in volume, the earth, and architecture. Spheres, cones, and cubes in bronze, his preferred material, gradually took over important urban spaces. Midway between faultless technical prowess and perfect implantation in their environment, Arnaldo Pomodoro's works are connected to feelings and contrasts. The smooth surfaces are broken up with lesions, a sort of implosion which reveals an internal, mechanical magma. Whether it is miniature jewelry or monumental sculptures, Arnaldo Pomodoro gives his work a geological aspect similar to a process of corrosion.
He uses the technique of lost-wax casting to make his jewelry. Often, necklaces and bracelets consist of many small sculptures, all quite different and worked on one by one in gold, silver, bronze, and vermeil. As for his

Untitled, 1989
Necklace
Gold, length: 52¾ in. (134 cm)
28/30, edition Artcurial
Diane Venet collection

pendants, they harbor a multitude of signs in their center, the secret writings of their creator. Arnaldo Pomodoro collaborated with the editors Gem Montebello, then with Artcurial, before reducing his production of jewelry to a very limited number of pieces intended for those closest to him.

Untitled, 1987
Bracelet
Gold, length: 7½ in. (19 cm)
7/30, edition Artcurial
Diane Venet collection

Untitled, c. 1967
Necklace
Belgium marble, 13 in. (33 cm)
Unique
Edition Gem GianCarlo Montebello
Diane Venet collection

Giò Pomodoro

Orciano di Pesaro 1930–Milan 2002

Close to surrealism and to abstract expressionism, Giò Pomodoro worked using materials in relation to space, mixing shapes that he discovered in antique pieces with modern mechanical geometry. He enjoyed using bronze, gold, marble, and plastic, most notably in the spectacular pieces of jewelry which he created with his brother Arnaldo. The first pieces of jewelry created by Giò Pomodoro in the 1950s were inspired by Byzantine culture, the Middle Ages, and the

Renaissance. The artist also experimented with contrasting surfaces, which led to a rendering of both smooth and rough finishes, that he called "surfaces under tension." The effect conveyed a phenomenon of growth and multiplication, obtained by his work with cuttlefish bone which he used for manufacturing the molds into which he poured

the metals. The jewelry of Giò Pomodoro is characterized by his expertise in manipulating the materials which he employed and the balance of his compositions.

In the 1960s, Giò designed models for the jewelers Fumanti in Rome, before collaborating with his brother-in-law GianCarlo Montebello, who set up Gem Montebello, a company producing limited editions of jewelry made by artists in Milan.

In the 1970s the artist concentrated on making sculpture and painting before starting a new production of jewelry in 1993.

Costa Coulentianos

Athens 1918–Plan-d'Orgon, France 1995

Costa Coulentianos began his career as a sculptor in Paris in the late 1940s. A graduate of the Fine Art School in Athens, and following a short stint in the Paris École des Beaux-Arts and then under Zadkine at the Grande Chaumière, he later encountered Henri Laurens, a sculptor whose influence was to prove crucial. In early 1950, he began to work in lead and welded iron covered in copper, tin, or brazed bronze, in a series of sculptures of acrobats. In 1957, he joined Hartung, Magnelli, Pignon, Prassinos, Singier, and Soulages in signed with the Galerie de France. Increasingly abstract sculptures all originate in a world of forms that are simultaneously lyrical, organic, and geometrical. An artist for whom substance is all-important, he preferred resistant materials, including iron, which tended to increase in thickness and dimension.

His interest in the human figure inspired several necklaces that pay homage to the women in his life. Influenced especially by Calder, but never reneging on his antique Greek heritage, he produced a large number of models in silver and polished brass: geometrical pendants, chains with interlacing motifs, and fans of identical pattern. The sheer power of his work almost transforms the human body into an accessory for the necklace, as against than vice versa. At his funeral the touching image of the many women filing past wearing one of his necklaces was unforgettable.

Untitled, c. 1990
Necklace
Gilded bronze, 4¾ x 10¼ in. (12 x 26 cm)
Unique
Private collection

Vassilakis Takis

Athens 1925–

Untitled, 2007
Necklace
22-carat gold, silver, diameter: 7 ⅟₁₆ in. (18 cm)
Unique
Naïla de Monbrison collection

The Greek artist Vassilakis Takis likes to explore the properties of all sorts of different materials. Vibratory movements, the displacement of centers of gravity, the use of magnetic fields, lighting effects, and repetition; all have been used as a starting point for his *Signals* sculptures. Having settled in Paris in 1954, he made friends with Yves Klein, César, and other members of the New Realism group. It was here that he worked on projects which became emblematic of twentieth-century sculpture, in the same way as that of Brancusi and Giacometti.

He created his first pieces of jewelry in the late 1970s, usually unique pieces. These first works were informed by the artist's research on magnetism: he arranged small balls of scrap metal, beads, and diamonds on a base of gold, copper, or silver, held together only by the strength of a magnet. In 1989, he collaborated with Editions Artcurial to create a bronze model of a watch, the face of which has a group of metallic pins lying across it, much like the needles placed on the breast of his sculpture *Magnetic Evidence* (1983). Takis then took to creating bracelets and necklaces, sometimes molded straight onto the body. Visual effects and movement, ever-present in his oeuvre, are harnessed by this self-taught artist to make his sculpture come alive.

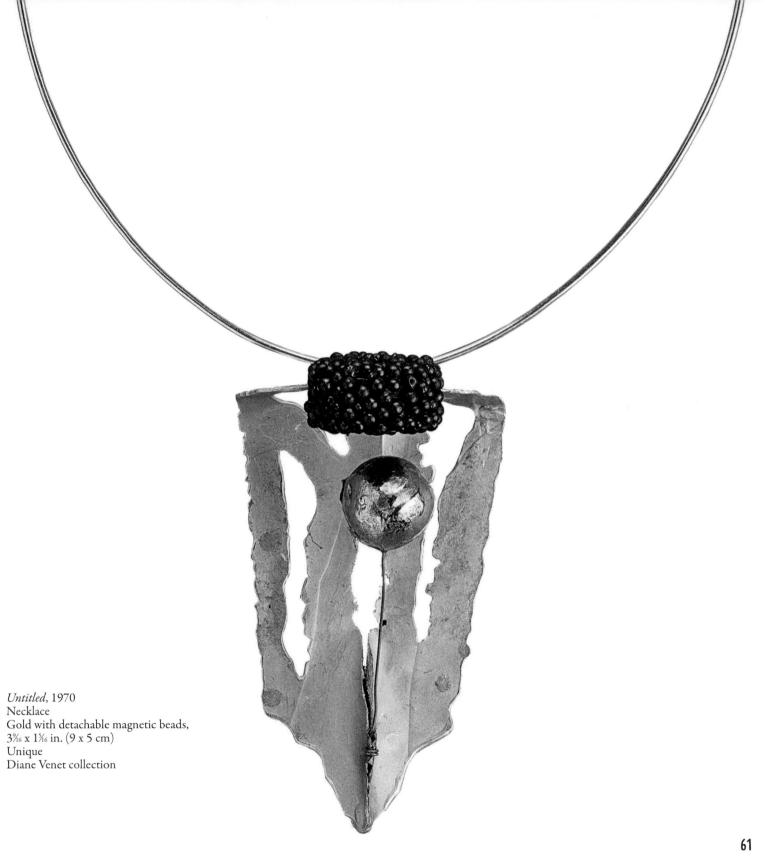

Untitled, 1970
Necklace
Gold with detachable magnetic beads,
3⁹⁄₁₆ x 1⁵⁄₁₆ in. (9 x 5 cm)
Unique
Diane Venet collection

Julio González
Barcelona 1876–Arcueil 1942

Trained as a metalworker, Julio González turned to art after meeting other artists such as Manolo and Pablo Picasso. He encountered the latter in 1897 at the Barcelona café Els quatre gats (The Four Cats), frequented by the artistic avant-garde of the period.

The artist first became famous for producing jewelry with his brother, for which he won awards. In 1892, he received the gold medal at the International Exhibition of Decorative Arts in Barcelona, and in 1893 the bronze medal at the World's Columbian Exhibition in Chicago. In 1914 he exhibited more jewelry at the Salon of Independents, some fourteen years after his definitive installation in Paris.

González, very close to abstraction and the surrealists, quickly went on to privilege the use of iron in his sculpture. His philosophy of using emptiness to create volume led to his being considered as the father of contemporary iron sculpture, inspiring other artists such as David Smith and Eduardo Chillida. At the end of the 1930s, because of the war, he was deprived of his material of predilection. He returned to drawing and painting until his death in 1942.

Collar, c. 1933–40
Necklace
Silver, length: 14 in. (35.5 cm), diameter: 7⅟₁₆ in. (18 cm)
IVAM-Valencia collection

Victor Vasarely

Pécs 1908–Paris 1997

Victor Vasarely invented his own pictorial vocabulary based on the union of forms and colors assembled according to his knowledge of optical science. During his training at the Mühely Academy of Budapest he studied architecture and discovered Josef Albers's research concerning color and perception of depth. From 1944, having worked for about ten years as a graphic designer in Paris, he concentrated on painting motifs obtained by a special graphic treatment provoking optical illusions. He is widely held to be the father-figure of Op Art through his visual kinetic images—geometric-based abstract art. The kinetic aspect of his work led him to apply for the patent for his "unités plastiques."

The two models of jewelry which he designed in the 1980s are in the same spirit as his painting. They consist of a matching set of a bracelet and earrings which Circle Fine Art had intended to issue as an edition of two hundred and fifty copies before going bankrupt. In 1985, he conceived a set that he baptized *Jolie* (Pretty), made up of a base of silver circles placed side by side, each decorated with stripes of mother-of-pearl and black enamel arranged in a mathematical way to give an illusion of depth and movement. Vasarely also produced a pendant whose central squares of coral, lapis lazuli, and onyx, surrounded in a frame of gold, give the impression of movement in the third dimension.

Jolie, c. 1985
Bracelet and earrings
Silver, enamel, mother-of-pearl,
6¼ x 1½ x 1$^{15}/_{16}$ in.
and ¾ x $^{15}/_{16}$ x $^{15}/_{16}$ in.
(16 x 4 x 5 cm and 2 x 2.3 x 1 cm)
113/250 (bracelet)
and 34/250 (earrings)
Diane Venet collection

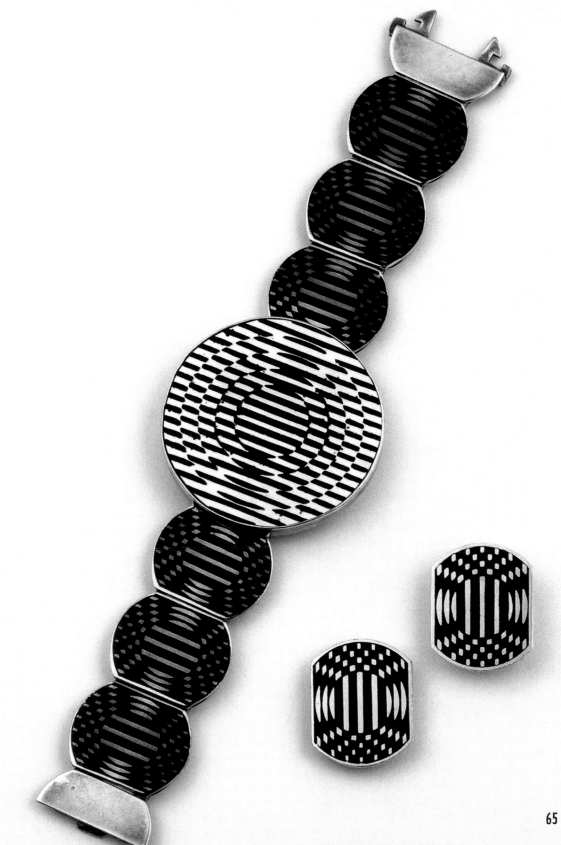

Tapio Wirkkala
Hanko 1915–Helsinki 1985

Finnish designer Tapio Wirkkala believed in the importance of manipulating the materials used for his works with the deepest respect for their integrity. Even when producing a series of works, the artist remained ever-present, modeling personally the pieces he had conceived, or at the very least being present during their assembly. At the end of World War II, he participated in the movement to beautify everyday objects, the principle of which he applied in particular to the art of glass making. Thus he declared in 1981 in the magazine *Domus*, created by his colleague and friend Giò Ponti: "My artistic world [...] is the shape of my way of life and of working. It grows through experiences, which are the ones of the daily life of people living in the North." Designer at the factory of Kahula-Littala from 1947, he became director of the Central School of Industrial Arts of Helsinki in 1951 before establishing his own design studio in 1955. In the 1960s, Tapio Wirkkala concentrated more on the creation of large-scale reliefs elaborated from plywood, then later bronze and wooden sculptures, sometimes of birds.

In 1970, he conceived models of necklaces and earrings named *Hopeakuu (Silver Moon)*. These pieces take their concentric forms from antique jewelry whilst their articulation echoes the principles of the modernity of the 1970s. Circles of various widths are maintained by a central axis which permits the pieces to oscillate depending on the movement of the body. His jewelry was produced in hallmarked sterling silver by the Finnish editor Nilo Westerback.

Hopeakuu (Silver Moon), 1970
Necklace and earrings
Silver, necklace height: 10¼ in. (26 cm), earrings diameter: 1 ³⁄₁₆ in. (3 cm)
Edition Nilo Westerback
Diane Venet collection

67

Eduardo Chillida

Donostia 1924–San Sebastián 2002

Nicknamed "the blacksmith" because of his passion for metalwork, Eduardo Chillida also designed monumental sculptures in corten steel, concrete, iron, wood, and granite. In the 1950s, he met the sculptors Brancusi and Tapiés, whose influence led him to produce abstract sculpture. Movement, the relation between man and nature, and the sea, are recurring themes in his work, which can be found in countless public spaces. Eduardo Chillida was also a trained architect, which explains the important part that drawing and engraving play in his work.

Fascinated by speed, Eduardo Chillida designed in 1966 a medal commemorating the memory of Saint Cristóbal, patron saint of drivers. In the 1970s, he created jewelry for those close to him, all unique pieces. He also produced a series called Abstractions, consisting of medals that were intended for his children. His next series of commemorative medals *Los Once de la O.N.C.E.* were made in 1985 for the Spanish national association for the blind. These are also metal plaquettes, produced with the goldsmith Francisco Pacheco, and characterized by the simple usage of hammered gold.

Abstraccion, 1977
Medal
Gold, 4 x 2½ in. (10.1 x 6.5 cm)
Unique
Museo Chillida-Leku, Hernani

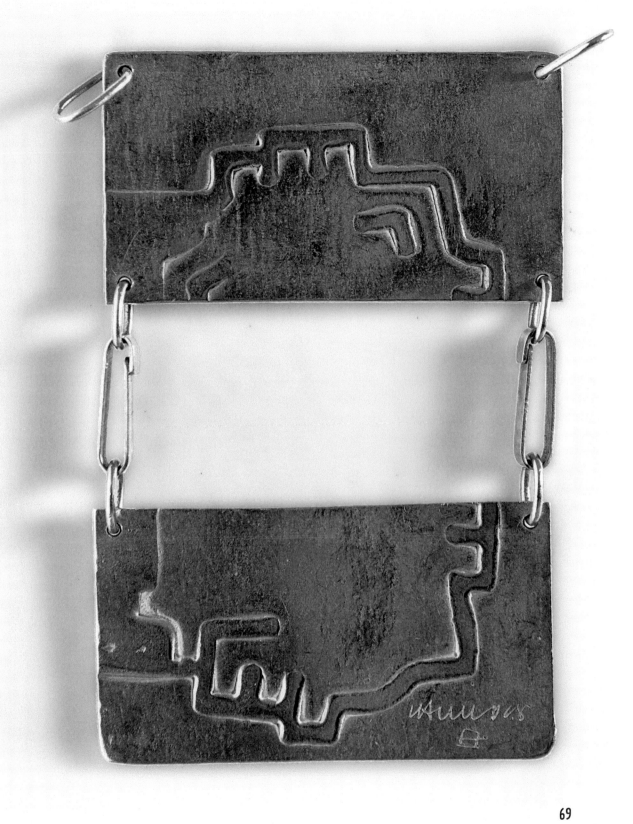

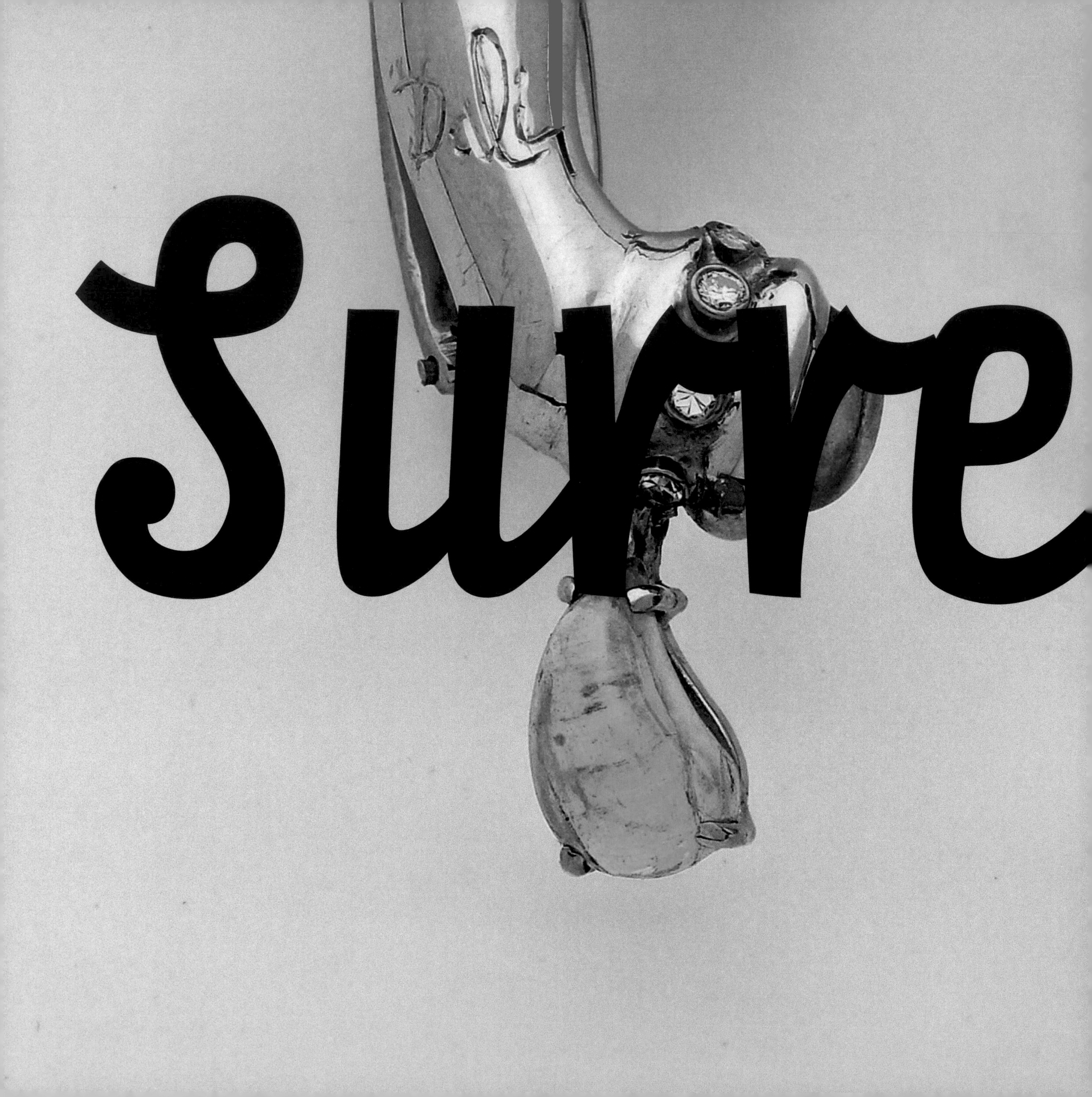
Surre

Giorgio De Chirico

Volos 1888–Rome 1978

Giorgio de Chirico, the inventor of metaphysical painting in which an illogical reality seems credible, settled down in Paris in 1911. He caught the eye of Guillaume Apollinaire, who from 1913 introduced the artist into his circle, presenting him to Picasso, Derain, Max Jacob, Pointer, Picabia, as well as Paul Guillaume, who became his first dealer. The onirism, the prophetic dimension, the subtle incongruities, and the originality observed in the work of Giorgio de Chirico found, from the early 1920s, a resonance in the budding surrealism derived from Magritte, Ernst, Picabia, and Éluard. In 1920 André Breton saw in the artist a creator of modern mythology in training, before accusing him of anti-modernistic regression from 1926. De Chirico later got closer to Futurism, and participated in the Italian pictorial movement Novecento. The controversy sparked by the surrealists did not prevent de Chirico from pursuing his work in a more academic vein, continuing to work on his paintings in his metaphysical style ad infinitum.

The jewelry of Giorgio de Chirico seems to emerge directly from his paintings. *The Small Muse* produced by Artcurial in the 1980s, made in bronze, gold, and silver, recalls *The Disquieting Muses*, with its figure draped in a classical style, which the artist painted in 1918. The pendant *Torso* is a unique piece, derived from the painting *The Uncertainty of the Poet* of 1913, which transforms into three dimensions the bust depossessed of its arms and head, belonging to the goddess Aphrodite.

Torso, 1970
Pendant
Silver, 2¾₆ x 1¹⁵⁄₁₆ in. (5.5 x 5 cm)
Unique
Anne de Boismilon collection

73

Max Ernst Brulh 1891–Paris 1976

Close to both the dada and the surrealist movements, Max Ernst made use of the absurd, of automatic writing, and invented the process of "frottage" (rubbing) and "grattage" (scratching) in his compositions with dreamlike components. Very prolific, Ernst used various media: lithographs, collages, paintings, sculpture (from 1934), and even a work in five volumes *Une Semaine de Bonté* (A Week of Kindness). His influence was enormous on the art scene in America, where he moved in 1941 because of the war, and in particular on the development of abstract expressionism that he inspired, along with Marcel Duchamp and Marc Chagall.

The collaboration between Max Ernst and his old friend François Hugo began only on his return to France. It wasn't until 1959 that Ernst sculpted his first models in Plastiline, handing them over to the goldsmith at the last possible minute, because of Aix-en Provence's heat in August, to be copied in gold. Altogether he designed a total of thirty-four pieces of jewelry; collectively called masks, they are each limited to eight copies.

These geometrical faces, often quite primitive in form, recall Ernst's recurring themes, in particular the painting *Éléphant Célèbes* (The Elephant Celebes) in 1921, which portrays the animal wearing a mask representing the head of a bull on its trunk. Brooches and pendants were embossed and chiseled: a long and difficult process during which the imaginary world of Max Ernst was conferred upon the jewelry.

Masque Ovale, 1976
Brooch
Gold, 2⅜ x 3⅛ in. (6 x 8 cm)
5/10, edition François Hugo
Diane Venet collection

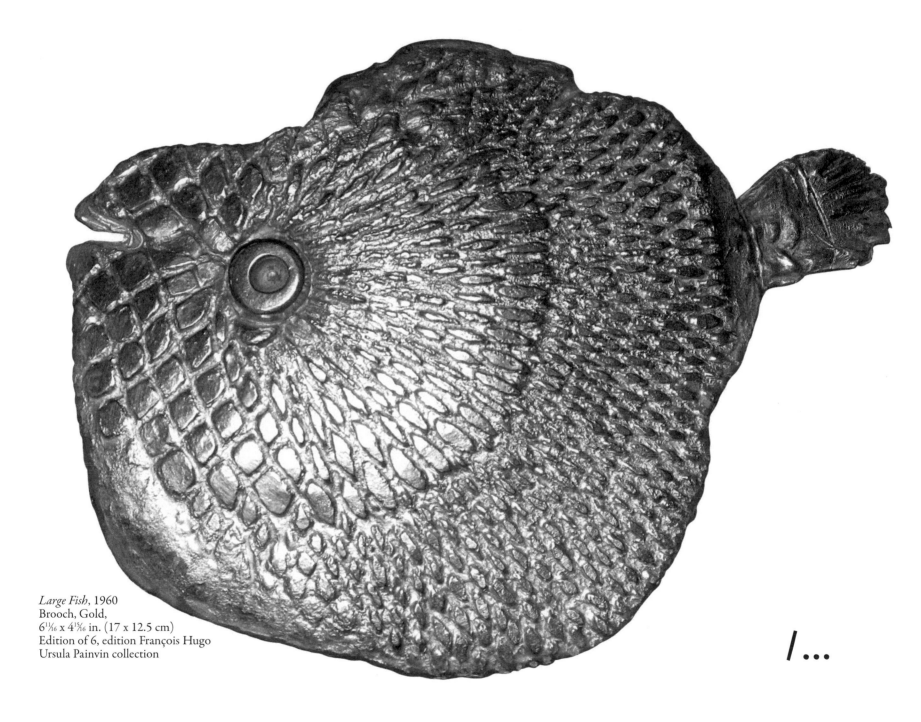

Large Fish, 1960
Brooch, Gold,
6¹¹⁄₁₆ x 4¹⁵⁄₁₆ in. (17 x 12.5 cm)
Edition of 6, edition François Hugo
Ursula Painvin collection

/...

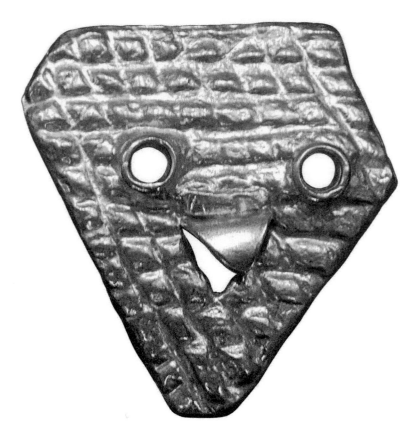

Tête Triangle
Brooch
Gold, 2⁵⁄₁₆ x 2⅜ in. (5.9 x 6.7 cm)
8/8, edition François Hugo
Diane Venet collection

Deux Têtes, Brooch, Gold, 2⁵⁄₁₆ x 2⅜ in. (5.9 x 6.7 cm)
4/8, edition François Hugo, Diana Küppers collection

Salvador Dalí
Figueres 1904–1989

The work of Salvador Dalí characterizes surrealism. He officially joined the movement in 1929 after his decisive meeting with the Surrealists: Tristan Tzara, Louis Aragon, André Breton, and Paul Éluard and his wife Gala.

His fascination for psychoanalysis defined his whole work, in particular due to his "para-noiac-critic method." The artist was inspired by his own psychoses and painted his most buried obsessions. He nicknamed himself a "poly-morphic pervert," approaching art through an intriguing erotic universe which turned the art world upside down. Curves and phallic representations—such as a rhinoceros's horn—came to life at his hands, and proliferated as his work developed. A provocateur, Dalí made an event out of every one of his appear-ances and quickly became a media phe-nomenon. But his first affinities returned to him during his exile in New York. He reconnected with Impressionism and worked with the iconography stemming from the sacred themes of the Renaissance. If the style changed, the notions of mysticism and duality remained constant.Dalí's jewelry pieces are among the

Lèvres en rubis et dents en perles, 1949
Brooch
Gold, rubies, pearls, c. 2⅜ in. (6 cm)
Audrey Friedman collection

78

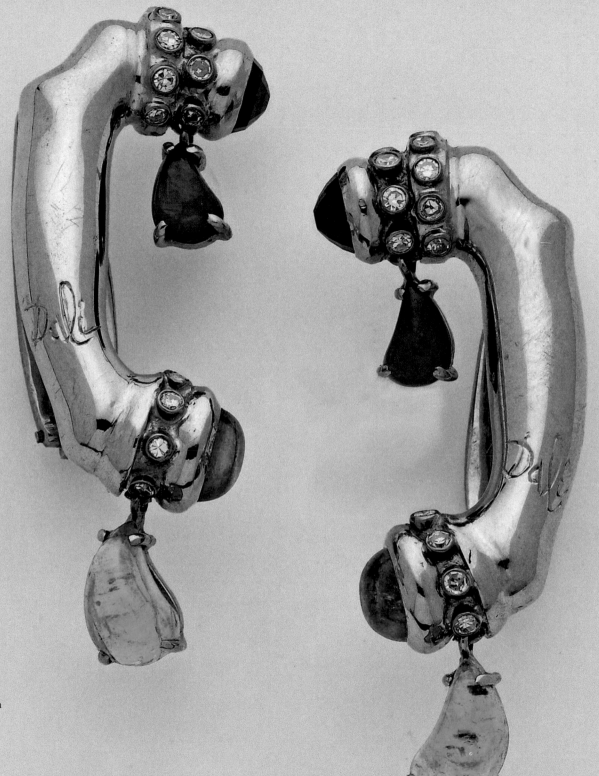

Telephone Earrings, 1949
Earrings
Gold, rubies, emeralds,
c. 1½ in. (4 cm)
Audrey Friedman collection

.../

most recognized in the world for their originality. After a collaboration with Elsa Schiaparelli in the 1930s, he made his own jewelry, using the most expensive means possible. His highly precious work was made possible by outside financing: that of the Finnish transport tycoon Eric Ertman. With financial assistance on this scale, Dalí could have as many designs as he desired made into jewelry by the Italian Fulco de Verdura and the Argentinian Carlos Alemany. Countless exhibitions of his jewelry were held from the 1960s, in particular at the instigation of the Owen Cheatham Foundation in New York. The works which he signed with his anagram "Avida Dollars" ("eager for dollars," the derogatory nickname given to him by André Breton) are inspired by anthropomorphic themes such as a mouth completely covered with rubies. They also bring to mind the well-known themes from his paintings: the brooch *The Persistence of Memory* transposes into reality the soft melted watch that rests on the branches of a decaying tree.

Belying his flippant appearance, Dalí reflected deeply about the place of jewelry in art: "Fulco and I, we tried to discover if jewelry was made for painting or if painting was made for jewelry. However we are convinced that they were made for each other. It is a marriage of love."

Gilberte, Brassaï, Dalí,
and Gala on a boat, Cadaqués,
1955

81

Man Ray

Philadelphia, Pennsylvania 1890–Paris 1976

Man Ray was a surrealist and Dadaist artist, alternately working as a photographer, film director, painter, and sculptor. In 1915, during his first personal exhibition, he presented cubist paintings. In 1921, the year of his arrival in Paris, he made the iconic sculpture *Cadeau* (Present), a household iron endowed with a protruding row of nails, highly emblematic of his sculpted work. But it was through his portraits and avant-garde fashion photographs that Man Ray became most successful. His photograph of Marcel Duchamp dressed as his alter-ego Rose Sélavy (1920) preceded the photographs of Meret Oppenheim, Picasso, Matisse, Braque, and Hemingway, as well as *Le Violon d'Ingres* (the woman in a turban with the drawing of the violin's sound holes on her naked back), and *Larmes* (the close-up of a heavily made-up eye with artificial tears falling), some of his most well-known images. Man Ray was also the inventor of a new technique of photogram which he named after himself: "rayography." Using this process, he introduced abstract motifs in varying shades of gray into his photographs.

The eight jewelry pieces which he issued in an edition of twelve copies between 1970 and 1976 with the editors Gem Montebello continued his surrealist themes. A close-up of a part of the face is seen in the brooch-pendant *Les Amoureux* (The Lovers), which takes the form of a mouth. His creative incentives were totally free from any of the aesthetic constraints of jewelry-making with his model for the ring *Le Trou* (The Hole). The long pink gold spiral earrings *Pendentif Pendant* (Pendant Pendant), designed to be placed over the ears to take the weight off the tall spirals, stemmed originally from a project for a lampshade he had produced in 1919. As well as these "objects of affection," he produced a gold mask called *Optic-Topic*, a small sculptural mask that hindered the vision, letting one see out only by means of two spirals of tiny holes, which was issued in an edition of one hundred copies.

Optic-Topic, 1974
Mask, gold, 3¹³⁄₁₆ x 7¹⁄₁₆ in. (9.7 x 18 cm)
79/100, edition Gem GianCarlo Montebello
Bernar Venet collection

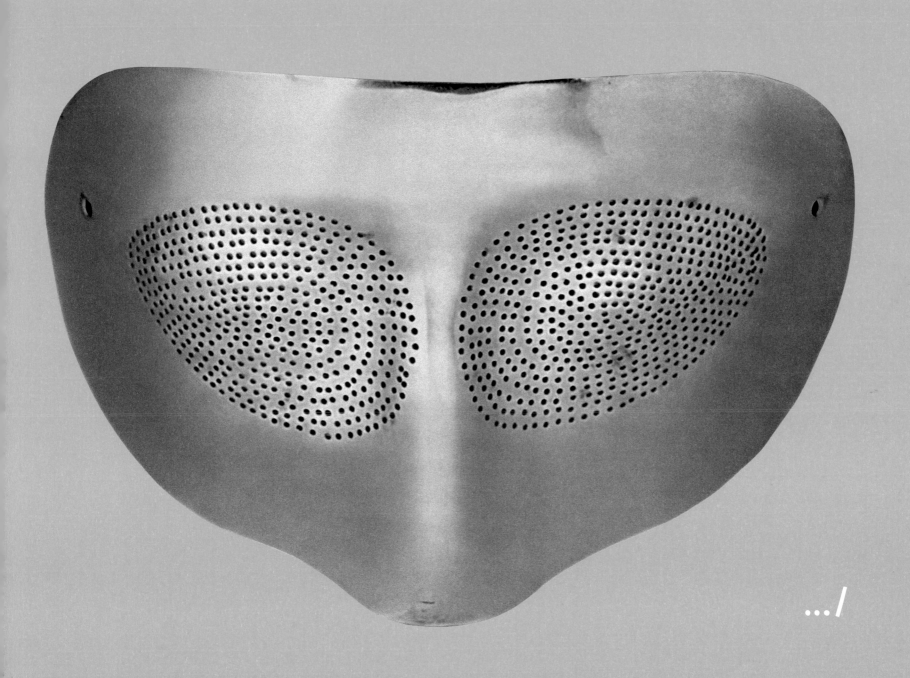

.../

.../Man Ray

.../

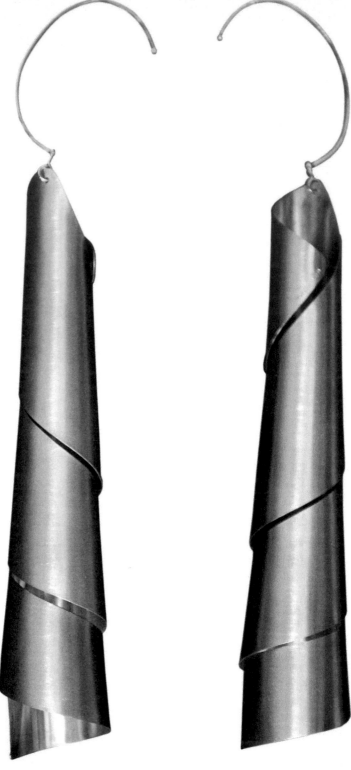

Untitled, 1970
Earrings
18-carat red gold,
length: 5½ in. (14 cm),
diameter: 1 in. (2.5 cm)
12 + 1 AP, edition Gem GianCarlo
Montebello
Margareta von Bartha collection

Preceding pages:
Left: Pendant, 1972, Gold, Sara and Marc Benda collection
Right: *Lee Miller au collier* (Lee Miller and William Seabrook) by Man Ray, c. 1929–32,
86 Photograph, Paris, Musée National d'Art Moderne, Centre Pompidou

Facing page:
Man Ray, *Le Trou*, 1970, Ring
Gold and platinum, height: 1⁹⁄₁₆ in. (4 cm),
diameter: ¾ in. (2.25 cm)
10/12, edition Gem GianCarlo Montebello
Diane Venet collection

Leonor Fini

Buenos Aires 1907–Paris 1996

Self-taught, inspired by her own imaginary museum, Leonor Fini expressed herself in compositions close to the surrealism of Max Ernst, Georges Bataille, Max Jacob, and Paul Éluard. She was also close to Salvador Dalí. She participated with the surrealists, without adhering to their group, at the exhibition Fantastic Art, Dada and Surrealism at the MoMA in New York, in 1936, and in a furniture exhibition at the René Drouin Gallery in the Place Vendôme in Paris, in 1939. Besides the theme of the cat, the dreamlike universe which she portrays in her paintings is populated with feminine or androgynous characters, sphinxes, and witches, all drawn with an unreal realism. The work of Leonor Fini became resonant with a somber atmosphere when she abandoned her adolescent figures full of innocence and introduced into her compositions a profusion of details and erotic elements in rich colors. In 1970 she declared: "All my painting is an incantatory autobiography of affirmation, the will to express the lightning aspect of being." Leonor Fini also realized countless portraits, among them that of Meret Oppenheim; illustrated many books, in particular those of Edgar Allan Poe and the Marquis of Sade; and worked on stage sets for the theater.

The necklace *Sujet en Or* (Subjet in Gold) produced in 1973 in eighteen-carat gold in an edition of twelve copies reuses the motif of horns that she had notably used in the engraving *Cat with Horns*. These horns can be worn as a tiara, torque, or pendant and are set in an onyx base as a sculpture. It was produced in collaboration with the editors Claude Tchou.

Sujet en or, 1973
Necklace
18-carat gold, 5⅚ x 4¾ in. (15 x 12 cm)
4/12, edition Claude Tchou
Didier Antiques collection

Leonor Fini, c. 1973,
photograph

Roberto Matta

Santiago de Chili 1911–Civitavecchia 2002

Untitled
Ring
Gold, 1 x 1 in. (2.5 x 2.5 cm)
Rosalind Jacobs collection

An architect by training, Roberto Matta spent his early career as a draftsman for the Parisian studio of Le Corbusier. During his numerous trips abroad, he met artists such as Henry Moore, René Magritte, Salvador Dalí, and André Breton, who encouraged him to take up surrealist painting. Very close to automatic writing, his *Psychological Morphologies* express by means of abstract images what the artist calls his "internal landscapes." Matta also investigated new techniques, and, in the 1940s, he used a cloth to spread his paint, organizing the composition of his canvases by this means. In 1939, he fled the war and settled in the United States, where he influenced a whole generation of artists, among them the protagonists of the School of New York. Having been excluded from the surrealist group in 1947, Matta expressed more and more vehemently his political beliefs in his brightly colored works. The Algerian War inspired him to paint, particularly *The Question, Djamila*, a work which denounced the torture inflicted on prisoners.

In the 1990s, Roberto Matta presented his first jewelry, expressing his desire to create "objects to touch rather than to look at, that I would like to invest with a sort of power to be transmitted by contact with the fingers, like some antique jewelry pieces such as amulets." This Chilean painter, who had been used to working on large-format canvases, was then able to work in gold, real pearls, and precious stones, but also ceramic associated with enamel for the creation of his pendants. The resemblance to amulets is striking, and we can see a kind of symbolic writing in the structure of Matta's jewelry.

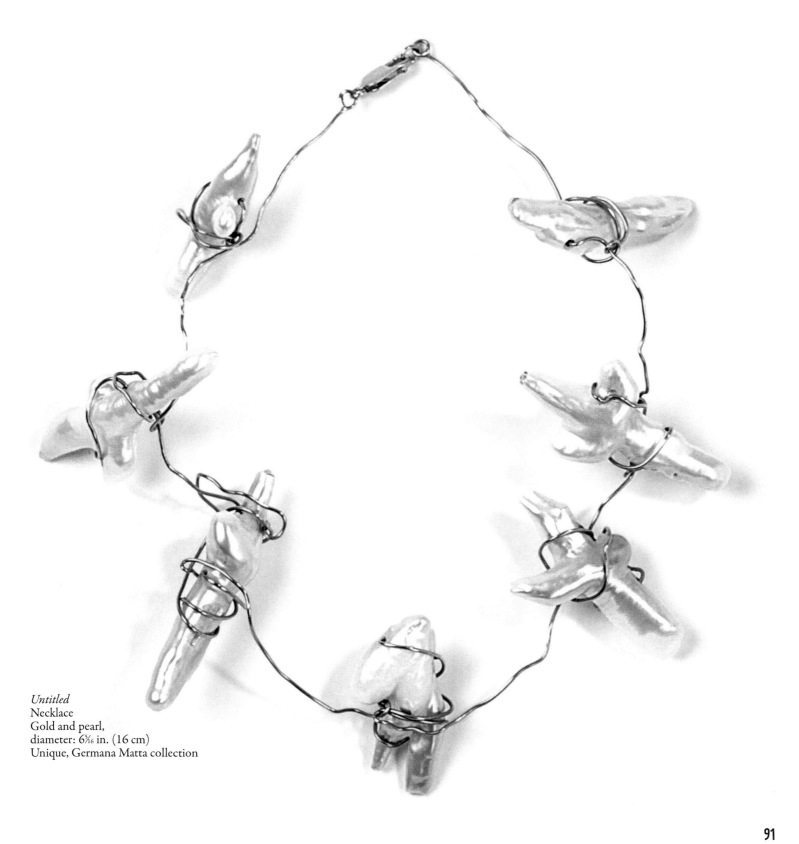

Untitled
Necklace
Gold and pearl,
diameter: 6⁵⁄₁₆ in. (16 cm)
Unique, Germana Matta collection

Jean (Hans) Arp

Strasbourg 1886–Locarno 1966

Poet, sculptor, and draftsman, Arp's work remained close to the Dada movement, which he helped found in Zurich's Cabaret Voltaire in 1916. Halfway between abstraction and surrealism, the artist firstly used the principles of automatic writing and hazard in his collages. It was however his sculpture which enabled Jean Arp to assert his ideas, in biomorphic compositions made of plaster, marble, or bronze. He received the International Grand Prize for sculpture at the Venice Biennale in 1954.

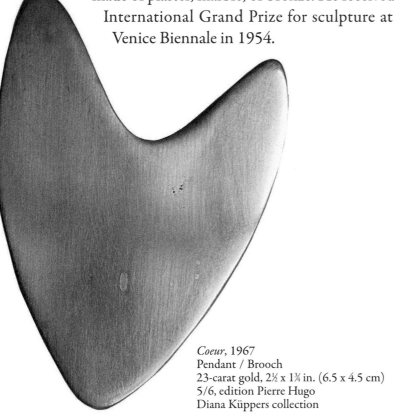

Coeur, 1967
Pendant / Brooch
23-carat gold, 2½ x 1¾ in. (6.5 x 4.5 cm)
5/6, edition Pierre Hugo
Diana Küppers collection

The use of jewelry in Jean Arp's work came rather late. Apart from his silver ring *Nombril* (Navel), created in 1918 for his wife, the artist Sophie Tauber-Arp, it wasn't until the 1950s that he started his collaboration with François Hugo, who was working at the time with his friend Max Ernst. But Jean Arp was wary of using gold, thinking the precious metal risked overshadowing his designs. His reticence led to him discovering a special finish named "eggshell" which gave a matte effect to his jewelry and made it seem less precious.

His brooch-pendants *Coeur* (Heart) and *Pique* (Spade), made in twenty-three-carat gold, are perfect examples of his attention to the cut and polishing of the material, making the object into a more graceful form with its soft contours.

Another significant piece in the artist's work is the necklace *Tête de bouteille et moustache* (Head of Bottle and Moustache), with its biomorphic shape. The motif, which he used as early as 1925 in a wooden relief named *Les Moustaches*, along with bowler hats and various walking sticks, humorously denounces the postwar bourgeoisie. This necklace, created in an edition of a hundred in 1960, was drawn by Arp to help Johanaan Peter meet the needs of the artist's village which he had established in Ein Hod, Israel, in the 1950s.

Facing page: Jean (Hans) Arp, *Pique*, 1967, Pendant / Brooch, Gold, 2¹³⁄₁₆ x 1⅞ in. (7.2 x 4.8 cm) AP 1/2, edition Pierre Hugo, Diane Venet collection

Jean Cocteau

Maisons-Laffitte 1889–Milly-la-Forêt 1963

Famous for directing avant-garde movies, Jean Cocteau was also an artist, playwright, and poet. His work is closely linked to his passion for mythology and his film *Orpheus* reveals him at his most poetic, subtly mixing myths and reality. In the 1930s, Jean Cocteau created pieces of jewelry for Elsa Schiaparelli, Chanel, and Fred. He was also the initiator of the Cartier Trinity rings (three bands symbolizing love, friendship, and loyalty).

In 1958, during a stay at Villefranche-sur-Mer, Cocteau produced his first pieces of jewelry at the ceramics factory Madeline-Jolly. He shaped white and red baked terracotta into the shape of fauns or astrological signs, unique pieces that he then decorated with a "tattooed drawing" as he put it. In the early 1960s, Cocteau decided to supply drawings to François Hugo: together they created thirteen pieces of jewelry, some sculpted as flat pieces in twenty-three-carat chased gold, some in eighteen-carat gold surrounded with precious stones. Many are human profiles in unusual forms decorated with fine lines, inspired by ancient cultures. The jewelry of Jean Cocteau was exhibited in 1961 at the International Exhibition of Modern Jewellery in London. During the 1990s, Anne Madeline, the daughter of Philippe Madeline and Marie-Madeleine Jolly, made posthumous jewelry following drawings left by the artist.

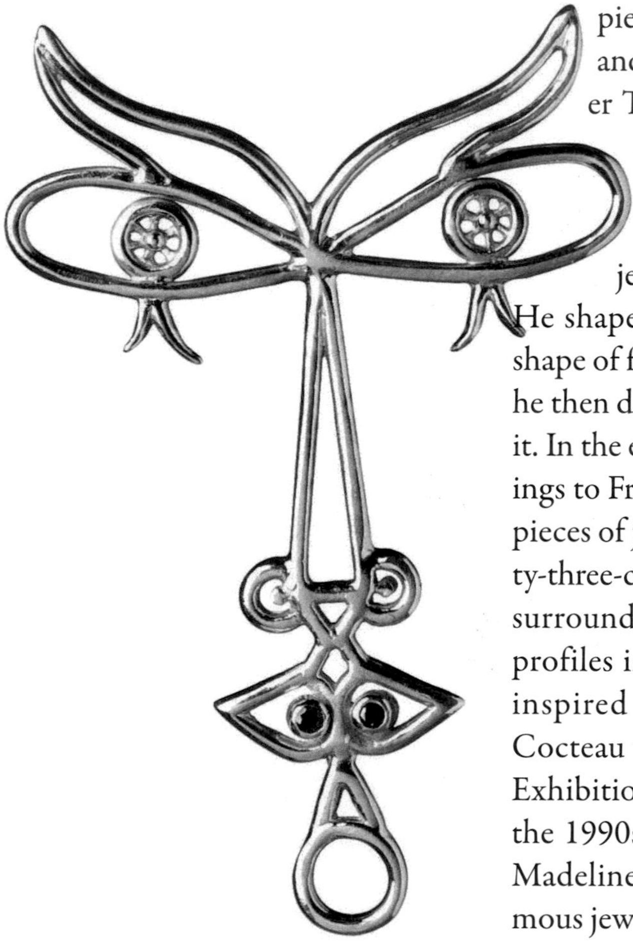

Madame, c. 1960
Pendant
Gold, rubies, and diamonds,
3½ x 2¼ in. (8.8 x 5.6 cm)
18/50
Diane Venet collection

Confidence
Bracelet
Gilded bronze,
Height: 3⅛ in. (8 cm)
Barbara Tober collection

Dorothea Tanning Galesburg, Illinois, 1910–

The exhibition Fantastic Art: Dada and Surrealism shown at MoMA, New York in 1936 inspired the former commercial artist Dorothea Tanning to new heights of creativity. In the 1940s, she was interested in the unconscious and the work of André Breton, and met several European artist refugees who had fled the Nazis to settle in the United States. In 1942, Max Ernst visited her studio and started a game of chess with her. In 1946, they married and spent thirty-four years together, mostly in France. The year of her hundredth birthday in 2010 was marked by several exhibitions worldwide.

Her work changed radically in the middle of the 1950s. She composed young women in intriguing positions, exposing a sexuality and female fantasy unimpeded by men. The brooch *Miss Octopus* reveals the erotic potential of the creature associated with feminine control. Dorothea Tanning's jewelry represents clouds, hearts, or totems symbolizing a woman's body and other artistic themes close to the heart of their creator, who was also a poet. These small sculptures, originally intended for people close to her, were made in the 1960s at François Hugo's workshop.

Miss Octopus, 1966, Brooch
23-carat gold,
2⅜ x 2¼ in. (5.9 x 5.6 cm)
3/17, edition François Hugo
Diane Venet collection

Facing page: Robert Motherwell, *Dorothea Tanning, Amagansett, New York*, 1945

Wilfredo Lam

Sagua la Grande 1902–Paris 1982

Close to cubism and surrealism, Wilfredo Lam was the most celebrated Cuban painter of the twentieth century. Of Afro-Chinese origin and touched by the santería religion (the faith of Niger adopted by the African slaves of Cuba), his work sits at a cultural interchange between European modernism and ancient traditions. The artist traveled enormously: studying first in the workshop of the reactionary painter Fernando Álvarez de Sotomayor, a teacher of Salvador Dalí in Madrid. He then stayed in Martinique where he was influenced by the ideas of the poet Aimé Césaire, whose verses he illustrated with numerous engravings in the 1960s. He settled down in Paris after World War II, befriending Picasso and the surrealists. He went frequently to Italy, where he started producing ceramics from 1975. The paintings of Wilfredo Lam represent luxuriant jungles and emblematic half-man, half-beast characters. The artist tried, by his artistic approach, to denounce the abuse caused by mercantile and colonialist societies, by painting what he called "the drama of his country."

In 1972, on the occasion of his exhibition Aurea, organized at the Palazzo Strozzi in Florence, Wifredo Lam presented ten pieces of jewelry, all unique pieces, inspired by motifs from his paintings. They are realized in three colored golds, silver, and horsehair, with the collaboration of Annamaria di Genaro. At the end of his life, although partially paralyzed due to a stroke, he continued to create, collaborating with the editors Artcurial for the realization of a limited edition of two pendants: *Water Bird*, in silver and blue enamel, and *Yemaya* in gilded bronze.

Zambezia Zambezia, 1972
Pendant
18-carat white, yellow, and rose gold,
height: 6½ in. (16.5 cm)
Unique, edition Annamaria di Gennaro
Didier Antiques collection

Jacques Lipchitz

Druskininkai 1891 – Capri 1973

In 1909, having studied engineering, the Lithuanian artist Jacques Lipchitz settled in Paris to attend simultaneously the École des Beaux Arts and the Académie Julian. He met the artistic avant-garde of the time, Henri Matisse, Juan Gris, Pablo Picasso, and Amadeo Modigliani, and it was this artistic buzz that influenced the beginnings of Lipchitz's career. Cubism fascinated him, and from 1915 he was inspired to create angular abstract sculptures which were exhibited at his first major solo show at the gallery L'Effort Moderne, Paris in 1920. In 1925, he created the Transparent series of sculptures using more naturalistic compositions, in which he played with bronze and the void. In 1941, he fled the war and settled in the United States. The jagged edges disappear from his sculpture, leaving work with curves and smoother surfaces. Little by little, the artist turned toward mythological or biblical themes, reinventing constructions already treated in the past, but this time in works filled with movement. In the 1960s, his works became impregnated with a wild baroque style scattered with cubist references. In 1940 he created a unique piece, a silver bracelet with small spheres of coral. He repeated this experiment at the end of 1960s and the beginning of 1970s, making three models of brooches with the aim of raising funds for the state of Israel. These pieces are issued in gilded bronze by Multiples Inc., and represent episodes of the Old Testament and different forms of the menorah, with the presence of animals, as in his sculpted work.

Untitled, 1940
Bracelet
Coral and silver, box front: 1⅜ in. (3.5 cm),
interior diameter: 1¹⁵⁄₁₆ in. (5 cm)
Unique
Diane Venet collection

René Magritte

Lessines 1898–Brussels 1967

The surrealist painter René Magritte is famous for his compositions full of humor and provocation, darkness, and even violence, in which he stages scenes from everyday life in an unsettled universe, transforming their original meaning. His 1929 work, *La Trahison des images* (The Treason of Images), with its accompanying sentence *Ceci n'est pas une pipe* (This is not a pipe) became emblematic of his work in its assertion that the image of an object cannot be the object itself.

His sculpture and painting *Le Prêtre marié* (The Married Priest), representing two huge apples masked in a cloudy no-man's-land, inspired the brooch created in 1990 by the Maison Wolfers, combining three major characteristics of Magritte's work: the surrealist background, the metaphor connected to the title, and the symbolism of the chosen shapes. Maison Wolfers, the highly reputed Brussels jewelry store, holds the rights to publication of all jewelry "faithful to the work of Magritte." They produced in the 1990s gold and diamond models representing the dove from *La Grande Famille* (The Big Family) and also three metallic spheres, the main subject of *La Voix des vents* (The Voice of the Winds).

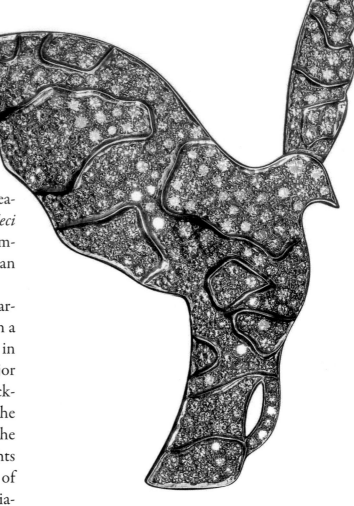

La Grande Famille, 1990
Brooch
Gold and diamonds,
2½ x 1¾ in. (5.5 x 4.5 cm)
Edition Maison Wolfers
Éclipse collection

Facing page:
Le Prêtre marié, 1990
Brooch
Gold and diamonds,
1½ x 1¾ in. (3.5 x 4.5 cm)
Edition Maison Wolfers
Éclipse collection

Baroques

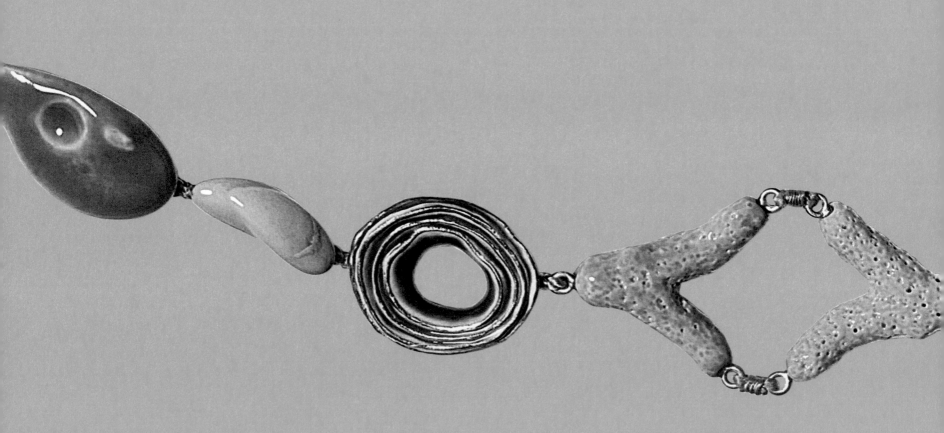

Marc Quinn London 1964–

A member of the group of Young British Artists supported by the collector Charles Saatchi, Marc Quinn, who came to public attention in the 1990s, does not hesitate to use provocation in his works. In 1991, he presented *Self*, a model of his head filled with his own frozen blood. He creates a discrepancy between his work and perceived reality by basing his explorations as experiments on the mutability of human and animal bodies. He uses an often shocking sculptural language to present a conceptual reflection on the human being's place in the world. He may use frozen blood or the placenta, as well as more conventional materials such as marble, resin, or gold. In the series dedicated to his friend, the model Kate Moss, Marc Quinn evokes the disappointment of man facing his image, separated from his internal identity, forever imperfect in this super-egotistical world. Whether it is by means of accomplished silhouettes or amputated bodies, he plays with paradoxes, and brings to light the illusions linked to our condition.

In 2007, he created for his wife a pendant representing a frozen strawberry. To indicate its immutability, and at the same time recreate the petrified aspect of the ice-cold fruit, he chose to inlay hundreds of diamonds on a gold base in the shape of a strawberry. For him, a diamond is an important metaphor because it is made of carbon, as is a human being, however, the diamond always remains ice-cold and timeless. There are two models of this pendant presented at the Louisa Guinness Gallery in London. One is made of white gold and the other in yellow gold, both of them are issued in an edition of ten copies. In 2009, Marc Quinn signed a unique ring entitled *Orchid Ring*, the reproduction of an orchid made in eighteen-carat gold, similar to his Garden series realized in 2000, when the artist congealed exotic flowers using resin.

Frozen Strawberry, 2007
Pendant
18-carat gold with yellow diamonds,
2⁹⁄₁₆ x 1⅜ x 1⅜ in. (6.5 x 3.5 x 3.5 cm)
Edition of 10, Louisa Guinness Gallery
Courtesy Louisa Guinness Gallery

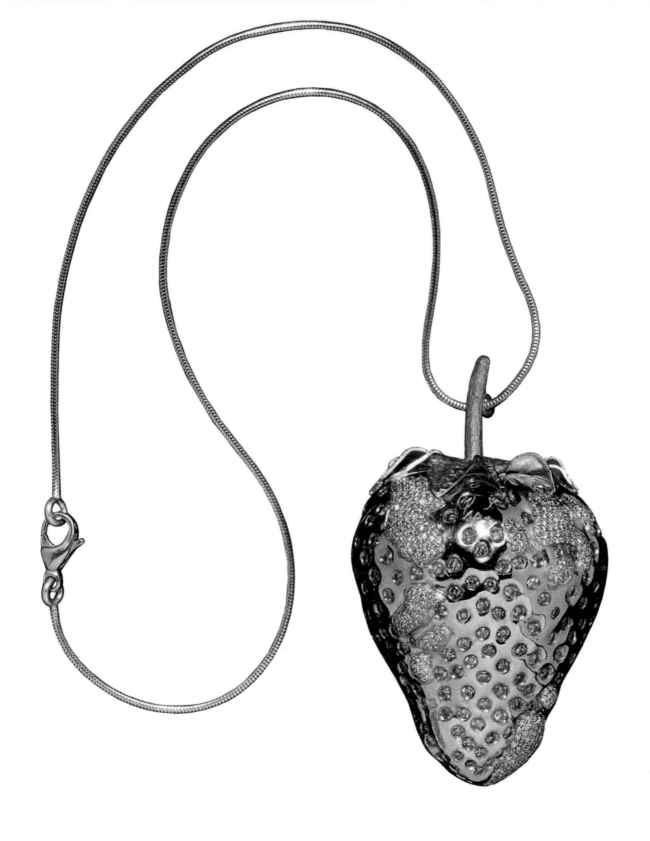

Ilya Kabakov

Dnepropetrovsk 1933–

Ilya Kabakov is an abstract artist who uses media as varied as painting, installations, drawing, theoretical texts, and children's book illustration. In the 1950s, he lived in Moscow under the Soviet totalitarian regime and began to create his first works known as "drawings for myself," works which did not progress past the stage of sketches. From 1980, he began to depict the everyday life of people in the Soviet Union, which he presented as a Utopia. In 1992, he settled in New York and started to collaborate with his wife Emilia on the realization of a common body of work. The themes of incompletion and abandonment are recurrent in their work.

The matching set of a bracelet and a ring, *The Fly*, made in an edition of fifteen copies, was produced by the gallery Elisabetta Cipriani. It is made of eighteen-carat gold, four pear-shaped emeralds, and nine brilliant-cut diamonds with enamel. These pieces of jewelry were originally designed in 1992 for his wife Emilia, but for many years remained at the sketch stage. They were eventually realized thanks to the Spanish jeweler Masriera, heir to the Barcelona jewelry store established in 1839, famous for its production of art nouveau jewelry and for its mastery of the difficult technique of fired enamel jewelry. The image represented in these creations is not without significance, the fly being one of Kabakov's most iconographic symbols; he first depicted it in his *Queen Fly* of 1965. It represents for the artist and his wife: "a symbol of freedom; it can go anywhere, be anywhere, unnoticed due to its apparent insignificance. Nobody can control the fly: even in totalitarian states, where everybody's life and movements can be limited and controlled, the fly is free."

The Fly, 2010
Bracelet and ring
Bracelet: 18-carat
yellow gold,
4 pear-shaped
emeralds,
9 diamond and enamel
brilliants,
2⁹⁄₁₆ x 1 in.
(6.5 x 2.5 cm)

Ring: 18-carat
yellow gold, one
pear-shaped
emerald, 3 diamond
and enamel brilliants,
1³⁄₁₆ x ¹⁵⁄₁₆ in. (3 x 2.3 cm)
Edition of 15, Elisabetta Cipriani–
Jewellery by Contemporary Artists
Ilya and Emilia Kabakov collection

108

Foglia, 2011
Necklace, Bronze and 24-carat yellow gold,
1¹³⁄₁₆ x 4³⁄₁₆ x ¾ in.(4.6 x 10.6 x 1.9 cm) (twig),
2½ x 1¼ in. (6.4 x 3.4 cm) (leaf)
Edition of 10, Elisabetta Cipriani
Diane Venet collection

Giuseppe Penone
Garessio 1947–

Giuseppe Penone was the youngest artist of the Arte Povera group in the 1960s. He concentrates his artistic activity on the relationship between man and the natural world that surrounds him. His empathy toward nature, and in particular trees, inspires him to integrate the vegetal world into his sculptures. The notion of cyclic time is also one of his preferred themes. Seeing equal importance in the process of creation as in the work itself, Penone highlights the analogies between man and nature. To create his first *Tree* in 1969, he carefully carved into a beam of wood, following the knots, until discovering its form at its twenty-second year of growth. By correlating this action with his own age at the same time, Giuseppe Penone proves that both are made up of their own lines, of which the imprint somehow or other is reproduced, linking us to the world of nature.

In 2011, he created the necklace *Foglia* (Leaf), issued in an edition of ten copies by the Elisabetta Cipriani Gallery. This piece is made up of a twenty-four-carat gold leaf on which the artist has printed the lines of his own hand. The leaf was then rolled around a bronze twig. This sculpture expresses the artist's idea according to which "the imprint of the skin, the lines of the hand, nails and veins draw, literally and metaphorically, a network that links us to leaves and trees, water and stones, animals." The necklace can be worn with either side facing forward and echoes the sculpture *Skin of Leaves* (2000), in which he questioned the theme of the imprint.

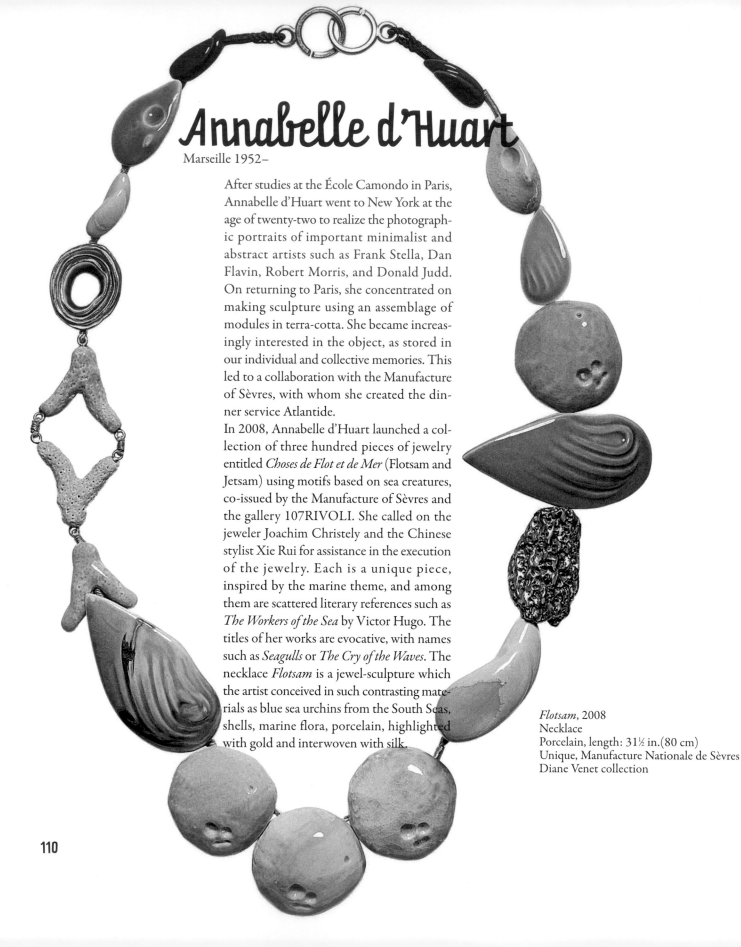

Annabelle d'Huart

Marseille 1952–

After studies at the École Camondo in Paris, Annabelle d'Huart went to New York at the age of twenty-two to realize the photographic portraits of important minimalist and abstract artists such as Frank Stella, Dan Flavin, Robert Morris, and Donald Judd. On returning to Paris, she concentrated on making sculpture using an assemblage of modules in terra-cotta. She became increasingly interested in the object, as stored in our individual and collective memories. This led to a collaboration with the Manufacture of Sèvres, with whom she created the dinner service Atlantide.

In 2008, Annabelle d'Huart launched a collection of three hundred pieces of jewelry entitled *Choses de Flot et de Mer* (Flotsam and Jetsam) using motifs based on sea creatures, co-issued by the Manufacture of Sèvres and the gallery 107RIVOLI. She called on the jeweler Joachim Christely and the Chinese stylist Xie Rui for assistance in the execution of the jewelry. Each is a unique piece, inspired by the marine theme, and among them are scattered literary references such as *The Workers of the Sea* by Victor Hugo. The titles of her works are evocative, with names such as *Seagulls* or *The Cry of the Waves*. The necklace *Flotsam* is a jewel-sculpture which the artist conceived in such contrasting materials as blue sea urchins from the South Seas, shells, marine flora, porcelain, highlighted with gold and interwoven with silk.

Flotsam, 2008
Necklace
Porcelain, length: 31½ in.(80 cm)
Unique, Manufacture Nationale de Sèvres
Diane Venet collection

110

Claude Lalanne

Paris 1924–

Claude Lalanne has been particularly inspired by nature, surrealism, and art nouveau. She often collaborated with her late husband François-Xavier, producing sculptural art mixed with design, working together without losing their individuality. The sculpture *Choupatte*, which she presented during her first exhibition in 1964, expresses the poetry and fantasy that typify her work. Claude Lalanne's whimsical universe was encouraged early on by the gallery owner Alexandre Iolas, followed by numerous orders from important collectors such as Yves Saint Laurent.

At first she produced jewelry using casting, stamping, and galvanoplasty. This last technique enabled her to "metallicize" berries and flowers, covering them with a thin film of metal. Next came the meticulous task of cutting and assembling, reinventing nature itself. For the most part they are unique pieces, in which the components dissipate to become sculpture, quite unlike traditional jewelry.

A further production originated in the 1970s, in collaboration with the publishing house Artcurial. These pieces of jewelry were made of bronze, copper, or gold, in the shape of butterflies, redcurrants, leaves, bows, and thistles. The necklace *Bouche* (Mouth) recalls her famous *Pomme Bouche* (Apple Mouth) where the artist placed an enigmatic smile on the fruit of the original sin, paying homage to Dalí and surrealism.

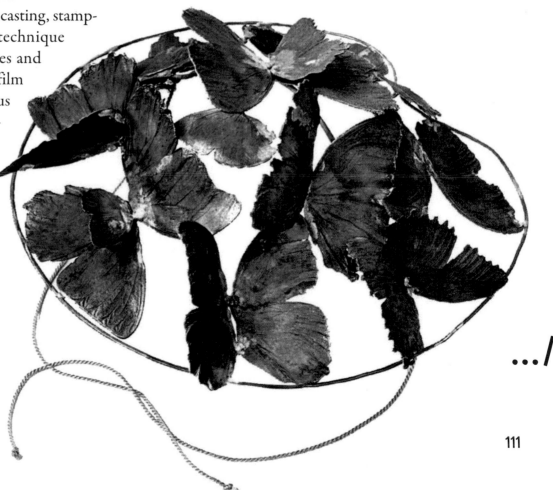

Chapeau Papillons
Headpiece
Galvanized copper
Louisa Guinness collection

.../

Seringat, c. 1990
Necklace and cuff bracelet
Gilded bronze
Rosalind Jacobs collection, Artcurial

Mimosa, c. 1990
Necklace
Gold, 7⅟₁₆ x 5½ in. (18 x 14 cm)
Edition of 30
Rosalind Jacobs collection, Artcurial

Grenouille à la Pince, 1998
Brooch
18-carat yellow gold,
4¾ x ¾ in. (12 x 2 cm)
7/8
Marina Filippini collection

Daniel Spoerri

Galati 1930–

It all began on October 27, 1960, when a group of artists met at Yves Klein's home to sign the New Realism manifesto. Among them was Romanian-born Daniel Spoerri, introduced to the group by Jean Tinguely, and whose work was still unknown to them. This was because the artist had only settled in Paris the previous year. Having fled the Nazis in 1942, he studied dance, a domain in which he excelled, eventually becoming the leading dancer at the Opera of Bern in 1955. It was some years later that he began to appropriate everyday objects, and in particular left-over foodstuffs, fixing them in time and randomly accumulating them: they are his *Tableaux-Pièges*. Throughout his career, Daniel Spoerri returned to variations on this theme. "Détrompe l'oeil," "pièges à

mots," "musées sentimentaux," or "cabinets anatomiques"; there was always an element of "suspended movement," as if an ongoing action had been abnormally and abruptly interrupted, or a souvenir brought to life. In the same way, the brooch *Grenouille à la pince* (Frog with Pincers), an item of jewelry created in 1998 with the silversmith Marco Filippini, makes reference to this process of turning everyday objects into works of art, a concept shared by the New Realists and the group Fluxus with whom Daniel Spoerri maintained close ties. Solidified forever in

eighteen-carat gold, this hybrid animal with the body of a frog and the pincers of a crustacean for a head, refers both to his *Tableaux-Pièges* and the *Conserves de Magie à la Noix*, a sort of lucky charm object whose only values are those placed on it by the beliefs of the person wearing it.

Kenny Hunter

Edinburgh 1962–

Scottish artist Kenny Hunter enjoys playing with the established criteria of sculpture. He reinvents forms with humor and boldness. Placing conventional subjects from ancient sculpture in a modern reinterpretation, he creates a kind of iconic dissonance. He often uses the animal shape, enriching his ideas with reflections on nature's adaptations to human encroachment. The sculpture *Like Water in Water* (2008), for example, represents a young deer stepping through a rubber tire. Noted for his sculpted busts, and his portraits using political figures, Kenny Hunter has investigated human history through his work since the 1990s. Combining materials in a subtle way, he masters structure and visual effects in a way that highlights all our uncertainties. He is also the author of two-dimensional works, inspired by the texts of Baudelaire, Marx, and Goethe.

The brooch *Rooks*, modeled in silver in 2008, represents four rooks, whose spread wings and introverted beaks form the second motif, that of the clover. Kenny Hunter here marries the image for good luck with that of misfortune, two symbols that are generally diametrically opposed. This piece of jewelry echoes the sculpture of the same name realized in black-painted resin.

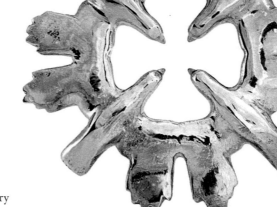

Rooks, 2008
Brooch
Silver, 4¾ x 5¹⁵⁄₁₆ in. (12 x 15 cm)
1/7
Courtesy Christian Scheffel Gallery

Magdalena Abakanowicz Falenty 1930–

In the 1950s, Polish-born Magdalena Abakanowicz started her studies at the Fine Arts Academy of Warsaw. At this time she produced huge format, brightly colored works. During the 1960s she transformed her style to use textiles, making thick weavings by hand from her canvases. She broke with the art world's traditions by suspending her art from the ceiling. These gigantic, three-dimensional original works were named *Abakanes* after her own name. Her interest for materials grew, leading her to fashion sculpture out of sackcloth, wood, resin, bronze, ceramic, and stone. For Magdalena Abakanowicz, the material was more than just a support, and became a means to reveal the unconscious. Her work is entirely dedicated to the human condition, a theme which she develops by writing metaphoric texts about the human brain. Her flexible works with organic forms find an echo in our feelings and the impact of our actions on our fellowmen. She also treats the theme of crowds in the Agora series, installed in a Chicago park.

When Magdalena Abakanowicz created the necklace *Cast of her Own Hand*, she selected a limb, in this case a hand, an image that she had previously used in several bronze sculptures, such as *The Hand* (2001). This unique example, created in aluminum, is the molding of one part of the body holding onto another, with folded up fingers reminiscent of a door-knocker.

Cast of her own hand, 2010
Necklace
Aluminum,
2⁹⁄₁₆ x 1¾ x ¾ in.
(6.5 x 3.5 x 2 cm)
Unique
Magdalena Abakanowicz collection

116

117

Damien Hirst

Bristol 1965–

The most well-known Young British Artist, Damien Hirst likes to push the boundaries of contemporary art. In 1988, whilst still studying at Goldsmiths College in London, he decided to organize the exhibition Freeze in the Docklands, a rundown area of the city. The show was a big success and propelled the artist onto the international scene. He then presented some totally original works such as the series Natural History where he used dead animals immersed in formaldehyde, medicines and pillboxes in display cases, and monochrome paintings decorated with dead flies, showing his credentials as a true master of provocation. But if his works shock, they remain no less charged with an important message that concerns the human condition: the ephemeral nature of life. As a conceptual artist he questions contemporary themes such as social problems, religion, pain, and ego, using a variety of media such as drawing, painting, installation, and sculpture.

In 2004, the artist created a white-gold bracelet in an edition of ten copies, in the form of a charm bracelet. From the chain bracelet dangle seventeen contemporary charms in the shape of seals resembling pills, a recurring theme of his work, associating art with science. This piece exists also in silver, in an edition of fifty copies.

In 2007 the use of precious stones in his famous work *For the Love of God*, the replica of an eighteenth-century man's skull set with 8,601 diamonds, represented an innovative foray into the world of jewelry. This initiative was followed in 2008, during the exhibition of *For the Love of God* at the Rijksmuseum in Amsterdam, by his collaboration with the jewelry store Gas, creating a bracelet with skull motifs: *Skull Gas*.

Pill Charm Bracelet, 2004
Bracelet
Silver, 8¹¹⁄₁₆ in. (22 cm)
Edition of 50, Louisa Guinness Gallery
Diane Venet collection

Gavin Turk

Guildford 1967–

Close to the "Young British Artists," Gavin Turk departs from the group in works that constantly interrogate the concepts of authenticity and value in the domain of art. Dealing in all sorts of materials, he is famous for his self-portraits: sculptures in wax or silkprints on canvas. The theme of self-representation is seminal to the approach of an artist who has developed a kind of double to whom he delegates the business of communicating his innermost thoughts. In addition, his oeuvre is freighted with references to the great names of art, such as Andy Warhol, Marcel Duchamp, René Magritte, and Yves Klein.

Introduced to jewelry by his father, who worked in the trade, Gavin Turk's output in the area was at the outset intended for his wife. It was for her that he designed a model for platinum earrings that proved much too heavy to be worn. In consequence, in 2004 he opted to use a lighter material in synthetic acrylic, a kind of resin that is cast into moulds made of pre-chewed gum – a process that imparts a highly individual appearance to his earrings, cufflinks, pendants, brooches, and tie-pins. For Gavin Turk, the medium of jewelry is capable of giving art a new lease of life.

Cufflinks, 2004
Cuff links
18-carat gold, resin,
⅞ x ¾ x 1³⁄₁₆ in. (2.2 x 1.9 x 3 cm)
Edition Geoffrey Turk
Courtesy Louisa Guinness Gallery

Tim Noble and Sue Webster

Stroud 1966– and Leicester 1967–

Tim Noble and Sue Webster, who came to prominence at the same time as the Young British Artists, are committed to a counter-culture society and through their work touch on themes of identity, sexuality, and the consumer society. The artists, partners in both life and work, collect garbage from which they assemble sculptures that are illuminated, creating projected shadows which transform to figurative silhouettes on a wall. They also execute works from neon and electric bulbs, making art from anti-art. Their first approach to jewelry is connected to their personal history and goes back to their meeting at Nottingham Polytechnic. At the time, Tim Noble was wearing a ring decorated with a skull which he had designed a few years earlier and had had made by his mother, a jeweler. Sue Webster admired the ring and Tim Noble had a new model made for his fiancée. In 2004 and 2006, the artists collaborated with Louisa Guinness, repeating the design of these famous rings.

They even reused the same mold that had been used for manufacturing their own rings for the realization of several series of cuff links, some in yellow or white gold, others in silver with ruby eyes (called *Skull 'n' Bone*), and a further pair in yellow gold with diamond eyes. Later this design would be copied for earrings. In 2004, they created the *Fucking Beautiful* necklaces and bracelets, derived from the sculpture of the same name, which Sue Webster considers dangerous to wear and rather provocative.

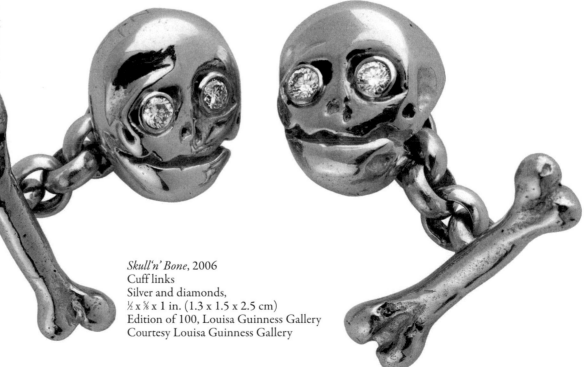

Skull 'n' Bone, 2006
Cuff links
Silver and diamonds,
½ x ⅜ x 1 in. (1.3 x 1.5 x 2.5 cm)
Edition of 100, Louisa Guinness Gallery
Courtesy Louisa Guinness Gallery

Miquel Barceló

Felanitx, Majorca 1957–

Miquel Barceló became successful early in his career as an artist in the 1980s. At this time, he produced drawings and paintings similar to abstract expressionism, and used the same technique of dripping as Jackson Pollock, whom he met in 1979. In the 1990s, Miquel Barceló traveled widely and began to incorporate sediments, hairs, sand, termites, and other souvenirs into his work, giving it an attractive third dimension. It was during a trip to Mali that the artist, who already used many different media for his work—from painting to sculpture, book illustration to collage—decided to create ceramics. This technique took an important place in his oeuvre, resuming his recurring themes of the passing of time, death, vegetal transformations, and human desires. The palette of colors became warmer and the forms similar to the motifs and landscapes of Africa.

In 2008, he decided to collaborate with the Spanish goldsmith Chus Burés. The artist started by drawing models to make as jewelry inherited from his marine repertory. *Boucle de Mer*, *Gousse Marine*, *Algues de Mer*, and *Hameçon et Appât* took shape a few months later, fashioned in eighteen-carat gold. Each model was issued in an edition of nineteen copies.

Hameçon et Appât, 2009
Earrings
Gold, satin finish, 4 x 1¼ x ½ in.
(10 x 3.2 x 1.5 cm)
2/20, edition Chus Burés design studio
Diane Venet collection

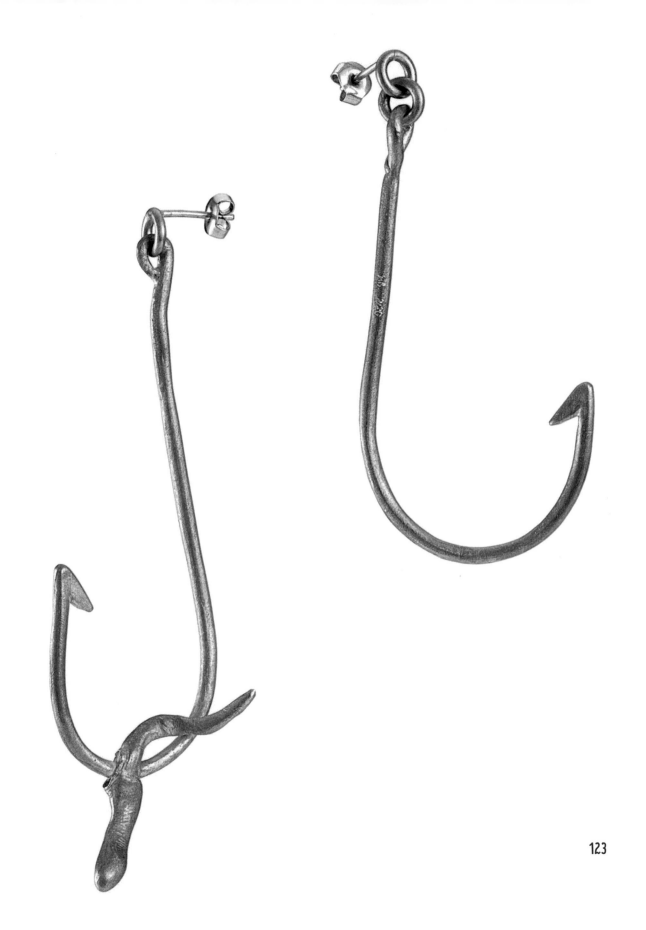

123

Louise Bourgeois
Paris 1911–New York 2010

Painful memories of childhood drove Louise Bourgeois to seek liberation through art. A mother who died too early and a father whom she considered tyrannical led her to try to exorcise her fears. At first Louise Bourgeois concentrated on mathematics, which she studied at the Sorbonne, before attending the École des Beaux Arts and the École du Louvre. Her departure to New York in 1938, following her marriage to the art historian Robert Goldwater, marked the beginning of her career, followed by her first exhibition in 1945. In the United States, she frequented the surrealists and began using very varied materials such as plaster, latex, fabric, and wood to create her *Woman Houses* and *Totems*. Louise Bourgeois's universe is particularly introspective, her works betraying her reflections on the unconscious, femininity, the family, sexuality, and the relationship to the human body.

One has an insight into the mind of the artist when looking at the silver choker *Barre de Métal* (Metal Bar) made by the fashion designer Helmut Lang in 2003, inspired by her 1948 design. It encloses the neck of the wearer as if to imprison or enslave her, yet remains decorative.

In the same spirit, the gold spider brooch reflects the ambivalence of the huge spider that the artist named *Maman*. Alternately protective and stifling, like the image of a mother... in this particular case, a mother who restored antique tapestries, the weaving of which makes one think of the web ceaselessly spun by the spider.

Gold Spider Brooch, 1996
Brooch
Gold, 4⅛ x 3⅛ x 1 in.
(10.5 x 8 x 2.5 cm)
4/6, edition Chus Burés design studio
Courtesy Louisa Guinness Gallery

.../

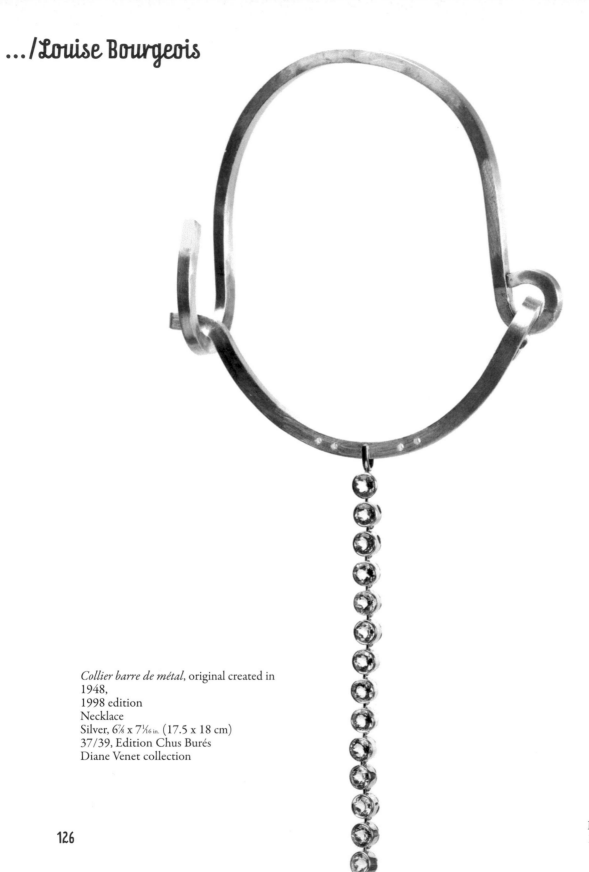

Collier barre de métal, original created in
1948,
1998 edition
Necklace
Silver, 6⅞ x 7¹⁄₁₆ in. (17.5 x 18 cm)
37/39, Edition Chus Burés
Diane Venet collection

Louise Bourgeois in the studio of her flat,
142 East 18th Street, New York, c. 1946

Untitled, 2011
8 rings and chain
Gold, calf leather case,
12⅟₁₆ x 1³⁄₁₆ x 1³⁄₁₆ in. (32 x 5 x 5 cm)
Unique
Diane Venet collection

Wim Delvoye

Wervik 1965–

An atypical neo-conceptual artist, Belgian Wim Delvoye raises numerous questions about society, whilst giving the impression of turning everything to derision. His work is fraught with contradictions, and his often shocking modes of expression reveal a pre-occupation with human behavior. In 2005, practicing vegetarian Delvoye launched a controversial debate on the exploitation of animals when he decided to establish a pig farm in China. The animals, bought from food-processing companies, are tattooed, exhibited, then later slaughtered and sold. In another vein, he exploits the use of religious worship to denounce the importance of the taboos inherited from our education. In 2000, with the first of the *Cloaca* works, he mimicked the work of a serious scientist by creating a digestive system that manufactured excrement. His drive to reduce cultural commonplaces to mockery places him among the most original contemporary artists today.

In 2011, he produced his first set of jewelry, consisting of eight rings, a chain, and a box, with all the elements intended to be inseparable. There are three different versions of this work, one in eighteen-carat yellow gold, the second in palladium, and the third in silver, each one being a unique piece, issued by Elisabetta Cipriani. Wim Delvoye uses, as in his sculpture *Jesus Twisted* (2006), a distorted figure of Christ on the rings.

Alberto Guzmán Piura 1927–

After his studies at the National School of Fine Arts in Lima in the 1950s, Alberto Guzmán started making his first, abstract, welded iron sculptures. In 1959, he benefited from a scholarship offered by the French government and settled in Paris. He began to work with new materials such as marble and bronze, making sculptures inspired by natural themes—light and sky, the earth and sand. The traces and lines which run along the smooth surfaces of his work seem to reawaken memories of the pre-Colombian art that he had so admired in his youth. Whether employing spheres, pyramids, ink drawings, or simple reliefs, Alberto Guzmán drew his inspiration from ancient cultures to elaborate a universal language, a kind of internal exploration through which he can diffuse his ideas about the world. Later, he extended his artistic repertoire to include stage sets, fountains, furniture, and monumental public sculptures.

Alberto Guzmán also became famous for his production of jewelry, adhering to his vision of "sculpture as a shaft of light." In 1992, he presented jewelry for the exhibitions Sculptors' Jewelry and Sources of Inspiration at Naïla de Monbrison's Parisian gallery specializing in jewelry made by artists. In 2006, he designed the ring *Mobile*, a unique piece in gold for Naïla.

Untitled, c. 1992
Ring, silver and amethyst,
1⁹⁄₁₆ x 1⁵⁄₁₆ x 1⁵⁄₁₆ in.
(4 x 5 x 5 cm)
Unique
Diane Venet collection

Gyula Kosice

Kosice 1924–

Gyula Kosice, a poet and sculptor born to Hungarian parents in Slovakia, has lived in Argentina from the age of four, and founded the Madí movement there in 1946 to promote concrete art (which favors non-representational geometric abstraction). He made wooden and metal sculptures to which were added articulated parts which the spectator could arrange. He was innovative in his use of neon tubes, then Plexiglas, in works characterized by their transparency and lighting effects. In 1949, he produced works heavy with symbolism by trapping water, often in movement, inside Plexiglas structures, inventing the hydraulic sculpture. He is the author of numerous monumental works such as the *Mobile Hydromural*, an aluminum, Plexiglas, water, and light installation made in 1996 for the Embassy Center in Buenos Aires. From 1946 to 1975, he concentrated on a Utopian work: the *Hydrospatial City*, presented in 1974 at the Espace Pierre Cardin in Paris. Numerous architectural models designed to house a community of people in space were suspended from the ceiling.

In 1960, Gyula Kosice transposed his research on the properties of water to the world of jewelry, and created the ring *Mobile Droplet*. This unique piece incorporates the artist's favorite materials, consisting of a drop of water imprisoned inside a structure of blue and transparent Plexiglas. This work is consistent with his production of luminous, mobile, abstract art that avoids all orthogonality. It is also reminiscent of works presented in 1975 during the exhibition Hydrospatial Kosice Jewels at the Espace Pierre Cardin.

Mobile Droplet, 1960
Ring, clear and blue Plexiglas, water,
1⅜ x 1 x 1 in. (3.5 x 2.5 x 2.5 cm)
Unique
Diane Venet collection

130

Jenny Holzer

Gallipolis, Ohio 1950–

Her *Truisms*, slogans plastered on walls and advertising hoardings in 1970s' New York, were the first works of Jenny Holzer. Her work, always connected with language, often qualified as feminist, is filled with irony, humor, and questions. The impact of her words, luminous messages created by means of LED, and sometimes associated with images, has led to her work being displayed in prestigious locations such as the Guggenheim Museum, New York, and public spaces in cities all over the world. The striking *Protect Me From What I Want*, or *It's Interesting*, lost on a black background, immediately involve the spectator. Writing became a fully fledged player in conceptual art.

In 1994, she designed a model of a silver ring for the art editors Parkett, consisting of seventy-five copies, twenty of them as artist's proofs. For the production of this project, she collaborated with the jewelry designer Patrick Muff in Cologne. She associated her image of a snake with the inscription of a hard-hitting sentence, which takes on meaning only when worn: "With You Inside Me Comes the Knowledge of My Death."

With you inside me comes the knowledge of my death, 1994
Ring
Sterling silver,
1⅝ x 3⁷⁄₁₆ x 2³⁄₁₆ in. (4.1 x 8.8 x 5.5 cm)
Edition Patrick Muff
Courtesy Louisa Guinness Gallery

Georges Mathieu

Boulogne-sur-Mer 1921–

Georges Mathieu began to paint in 1942 after studies in law, philosophy, and literature. He began to establish his style in 1947 based on the Lyrical Abstraction principles held dear to the painters Wols and Pollock. That same year, inspired by Tachism, the artist founded the group Psychique Non-Figuration with the poet and painter Camille Bryen. Georges Mathieu's works are peppered with characters in strong and brilliant colors: red, blue, black, and white are his favorite pigments, standing out against plain backgrounds. The titles that he attributes to his paintings, such as *Louis IX débarque à Damiette* in 1958, evoke his admiration for subjects of the seventeenth century and his desire to become the new Le Brun. Mathieu's ideograms allow the artist to create his paintings very fast and intuitively, leaving no place for the conscious intention of painting. It is these same signs, using a decoratively linear style, which lead to his being considered the first Western calligrapher.

From the 1960s, he created several brooches and pendants presented during the exhibition Antagonisme II, The Object at the Museum of Decorative Arts in Paris in 1962. Georges Mathieu used gold and precious stones to produce these unique pieces, exact replicas of his pictorial work. The piece presented here, dated 1970, is characterized by a gold base surrounded by a green tourmaline. In jewelry-making Georges Mathieu's prefers to use materials without too many alloys, just what is necessary for modeling the object. The artist expresses his desire to maintain his close relationship with his jewelry in these terms: "Until now my jewelry had only two dimensions. I dream of giving them a third. The ideal, you understand, would be to extract the jewelry directly from the gold."

Untitled, 1970
Brooch
Gold and green tourmaline, opaline,
4 x 2¾ in. (10 x 7 cm)
Unique
Ursula Painvin collection

Yue Minjun
Daqing 1962–

Yue Minjun portrays a stereotypical character with a wide, toothy smile and tightly closed eyes in all of his painted and sculpted works. This self-portrait, which by extension represents the Chinese population, constitutes a harsh criticism of this society, programmed not to see the reality of the world, yet all the while displaying an outward cheerfulness. Yue Minjun also uses this grinning figure in garish colors to express the lack of humanity and the violence of western society. He does not hesitate to appropriate the works of earlier artists, such as in his powerful work of 1995 *Execution*, inspired by the 1989 Tiananmen Square confrontation, where he reinterprets *The Executions of the Third of May 1808* by Goya and *The Execution of Maximilian* by Manet. Yue Minjun also attacks symbols of western society by parodying icons in such works as *Marilyn Monroe* (2000).

In 2008, he created the piece of jewelry *Doubleface Man* in association with the editors Filippini, echoing the characteristic, hilarious faces of his painted and sculpted works. The resulting brooch-pendant presents a double laughing face, made in yellow and white eighteen-carat gold, and is produced in an edition of eight copies.

Doubleface Man, 2008
Brooch
18-carat yellow and white gold,
2⅜ x 2⁹⁄₁₆ in. (6 x 6.5 cm)
7/8, edition Filippini
Marina Filippini collection

Louise Nevelson

Kiev 1900–New York 1988

In her youth, the Ukranian-born American sculptor Louise Nevelson had very diverse interests and experimented with many different artistic media. She studied painting, dance, singing, acted in European movies, and, in the 1950s began to work with bronze and wood. It was not until she was almost sixty that Diego Rivera's former assistant realized that her real passion lay with sculpture. Revealed to the general public by her New York exhibition Moon Garden Plus One in 1958, her work consisted of non-figurative creations produced in diverse materials such as Plexiglas, steel, and wood. In the 1960s, she worked on the series Environment, open free-standing structures, covered with black, white, or gold paint, on which accumulate parts of chair legs or elements of banisters. Marked by surrealism, cubism, and the primitive arts, she remained famous for her boxes, close to abstract expressionism, which she stacked on walls like a cabinet of curiosities inhabited by a play of light and shade. Louise Nevelson's items of jewelry are really sculptures on a reduced scale, and demonstrate the same creative drive as her monumental works. In the 1970s she created some unique pieces—brooches and necklaces—in wood and metal, sculpted and assembled by hand, and painted once again in black, white, or gilded, to which she would add found objects.

Untitled, 1985–86
Pendant
Painted wood on metal,
2⅝ x 2½ x 2 in. (6.7 x 6.4 x 5.1 cm)
Unique
Courtesy Friedman Benda Gallery

Untitled, 1985–86
Pendant
Painted wood on metal,
7¾ x 3¾ x ⅞ in. (19.7 x 9.5 x 2.2 cm)
Unique
Courtesy Friedman Benda Gallery

135

Orlan
Saint-Etienne 1947–

Besides her work as a painter and sculptor, Orlan has, since 1964, been the instigator of numerous performances that she calls "carnal art," the main medium of which is her own body. One of her first most memorable appearances took place in the middle of the 1960s, when, disguised as huge moneybox, she sold her *Baiser de L'Artiste* (Artist's Kiss) for five francs to whoever wanted one. Later she staged happenings dressed in extravagant or religious clothes, reminding everyone that a woman's body is totally subject to social standards. Through her physical actions she aimed to modify the notion of what is beautiful. Around 1982, having directed the international performance symposium in Lyon for five years, she published her manifesto *Carnal Art*. A long series of plastic surgery operations followed, all filmed and photographed, which she underwent between 1990 and 1993. She then turned towards biotechnology and created installations close to science, with *Le Manteau d'Arlequin* (The Harlequin Coat), a work constituted of an assemblage of a culture of her own cells and those of animals, plus skins of different colors, ages, and origins.

In 2010, she designed the model for a brooch named *Tête de fou* (Madman's Head) realized at the request of Diane Venet by the jeweler Patrick Boisgrollier. This work, in an edition of eight copies each in gold and silver, recalls the hybrid faces which the artist created from the 1990s by means of retouched digital photographs. This model of an African woman comes from the series Self-Hybridization. With this process, Orlan questions again the concept of beauty through different cultures.

Tête de fou, 2010
Brooch
Silver and gold,
3³/₁₆ x 4⅛ x 1⅜ in. (8.5 x 10.5 x 3 cm)
1/8, edition Arcas
Diane Venet collection

Anne and Patrick Poirier

Marseille 1941– and Nantes 1942–

The works of Anne and Patrick Poirier are connected to memory and culture by means of models, drawings, prints, and herbariums. Their common interest in archaeology has inspired them to create works halfway between historic reality and mythology. After a stay at the Villa Medici in Rome from 1969 to 1973, the artists begin to reinterpret history around the theme of burned-out cities. They created sculptures such as *Domus Aurea*, a reference to the Roman emperor Nero famous for playing the lyre while Rome burned during the fire of the year 63. In the 1980s, the couple erected huge collapsed sculptures, denouncing human pride by the realization of these deliberately destroyed outsize monuments. Anne and Patrick Poirier approach once more the subject of antique culture with their gold brooch representing an eye. The choice of this organ is not in any way arbitrary; the eye plays a dominating role in the beliefs of numerous cultures. It also echoes their marble sculpture *The Forgetful Eye* (2010). They were inspired by the discovery of many pieces of antique architecture, and particularly the gigantic marble eye capable of seeing the infinity of time in the *Valley of Mist*, in the grounds of the Domaine at Chaumont-sur-Loire.

Untitled, 1980s
Brooch
Gold, 2⅜ x 2⅜ in. (6 x 6 cm)
2/12, edition Gallery Eolia
Anne and Patrick Poirier collection

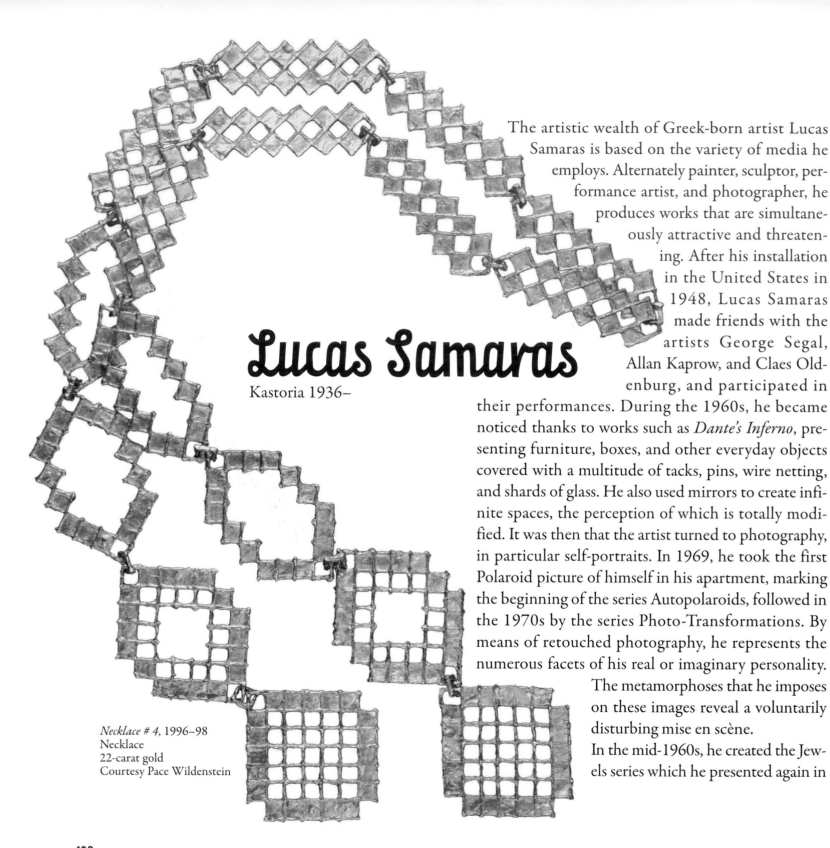

Lucas Samaras

Kastoria 1936–

The artistic wealth of Greek-born artist Lucas Samaras is based on the variety of media he employs. Alternately painter, sculptor, performance artist, and photographer, he produces works that are simultaneously attractive and threatening. After his installation in the United States in 1948, Lucas Samaras made friends with the artists George Segal, Allan Kaprow, and Claes Oldenburg, and participated in their performances. During the 1960s, he became noticed thanks to works such as *Dante's Inferno*, presenting furniture, boxes, and other everyday objects covered with a multitude of tacks, pins, wire netting, and shards of glass. He also used mirrors to create infinite spaces, the perception of which is totally modified. It was then that the artist turned to photography, in particular self-portraits. In 1969, he took the first Polaroid picture of himself in his apartment, marking the beginning of the series Autopolaroids, followed in the 1970s by the series Photo-Transformations. By means of retouched photography, he represents the numerous facets of his real or imaginary personality. The metamorphoses that he imposes on these images reveal a voluntarily disturbing mise en scène.

In the mid-1960s, he created the Jewels series which he presented again in

Necklace # 4, 1996–98
Necklace
22-carat gold
Courtesy Pace Wildenstein

Untitled, 1988
Ring
Diameter: 1³/₁₆ in. (3 cm)
Unique, prototype
Barbara Rose collection

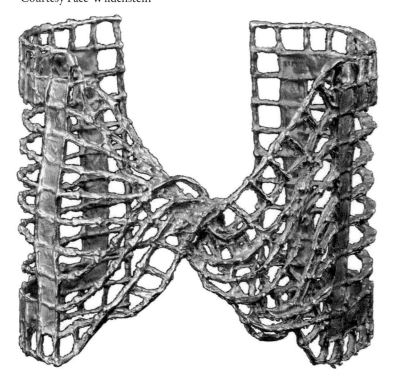

Untitled, 1996–98
Bracelet
22-carat gold
Unique
Courtesy Pace Wildenstein

2009 as part of his installation representing Greece at the fifty-third Biennale in Venice. It consisted of aluminum paper sculptures overlaid on a more solid support, representing the head, the groin, and the feet of the artist, a sort of unfinished self-portrait. In 1998, he also presented fifty-four pieces of twenty-two-carat gold jewelry at the Pace Gallery in Manhattan. The intertwined gold chicken wire threads on many of these pieces form a kind of grid, already seen on his boxes made in the 1960s.

Tunga
Rio de Janeiro 1952–

An architect by training, Tunga spread his artistic wings to take up sculpture, drawing, photography, movies, installations, and performance art. He alternates between an imaginary and a real world, introducing into his works countless literary, psychoanalytical, philosophical, and scientific references. The result is a poetic oeuvre the freedom and exuberance of which bring to mind the baroque era. Generally he is extremely exacting about the materials that make up his work, and mixes textures to obtain a perfect alchemy between them. The sculpture-jewelry *The Elective Affinities* (2003), testifies

to this process: huge steel molars are attached to and embedded in shapeless steel boulders on the ground, creating a balance in the composition. Later, invited to exhibit in a space beneath the Louvre pyramid in 2005, he succeeded in a masterful way in establishing a dialogue between two cultures. His work *The Meeting of Two Worlds* was a monumental installation consisting of iron rods, hammocks, human hair, steel ropes, skeletons, and skulls suspended from a gallows, which, when it rocked, led to a perception of the dichotomy between the hard and the soft elements.

This contradictory association ensures, for the artist, a circulation of energy.
In 2001, Tunga designed an eighteen-carat gold necklace, a one-off piece called *The Jewelry of Beauty and the Beast*. There is a prototype of *Beauty and the Beast*, a sculpture he made that same year in bronze, iron, and copper, which features the same crater motifs as the jewelry. There are also similarities with the conceptual drawing *Family Portrait: La Belle*, realized in 2001.

Les Bijoux de la belle et la bête,
2001
Necklace
Gold, 1⅞₆ x 5¹⁵⁄₁₆ x 4 in.
(5 x 15 x 10 cm)
Unique
Cordelia Fourneau de Mello
Mourao collection

Deer Pin, 2009
Brooch, Cast silver,
2¼ x 4⅛ x ¼ in.
(5.7 cm x 10.5 cm x 0.6 cm)
Courtesy Pace Wildenstein

Kiki Smith Nuremberg 1954–

The daughter of minimalist artist Tony Smith, Kiki Smith became well known in the 1970s for her feminist approach to art. She uses elements of the human body and animals to investigate notions of identity and their relationship to nature. Her sculptures also explore the perceptions of the body via formal associations which help her extract man's vital relationship to his environment. The scope of her work can be defined by her use of a variety of different media: sculpture, drawing, printmaking, and photography. Her works have a metaphorical impact. She is a member of the New York group Colab, whose interests revolve around a questioning of society from both a political and social point of view. Already an adept of changes of scale, as well as of the use of very different materials such as bronze, wax, or glass in her works, she then decided to experiment with jewelry-making in beaten silver, creating pendants and brooches. In her jewelry production we find a whole bestiary populated with birds, butterflies, or deer, associated with shooting stars and other naturalistic themes. The brooch *Deer Pin* created in 2009 presents a deer and a rabbit running in a natural space. In her jewelry as in the rest of her work, one notices the strong influence of folk tales, capable of transmitting a morality from the story told through her work.

Frank Stella
Malden, Massachussets 1936–

Untitled, 2010
Ring
Gold, 1¾ x 3¾ x 2 in. (4.4 x 8.2 x 5 cm)
Edition of 5, The Gallery Mourmans
Diane Venet collection

An uncontested master of the American abstraction which, at the end of the 1950s, continued where the generation of Newman and Rothko had left off, Frank Stella first exhibited his "Black Paintings" at the famous show, "Sixteen Americans," in New York's MoMA when aged just twenty-three. His subsequent influence on minimal art, whose practitioners learnt much from his "shaped canvases" which from 1961 had introduced the idea of system into the composition of artworks, is undeniable.

His oeuvre has constantly called itself into question, shifting from black to color, from picture to relief, from sculpture to architectural projects. Resistant at first to the area of jewelry, however, Stella finally presented a debut prototype gilt-painted necklace in a style inspired by his reliefs in 2009. In 2010, he collaborated with Ernest Mourmans and Marc Benda on a gold ring with curved forms, it too derived from his work as a sculptor, which was brought out in just five copies.

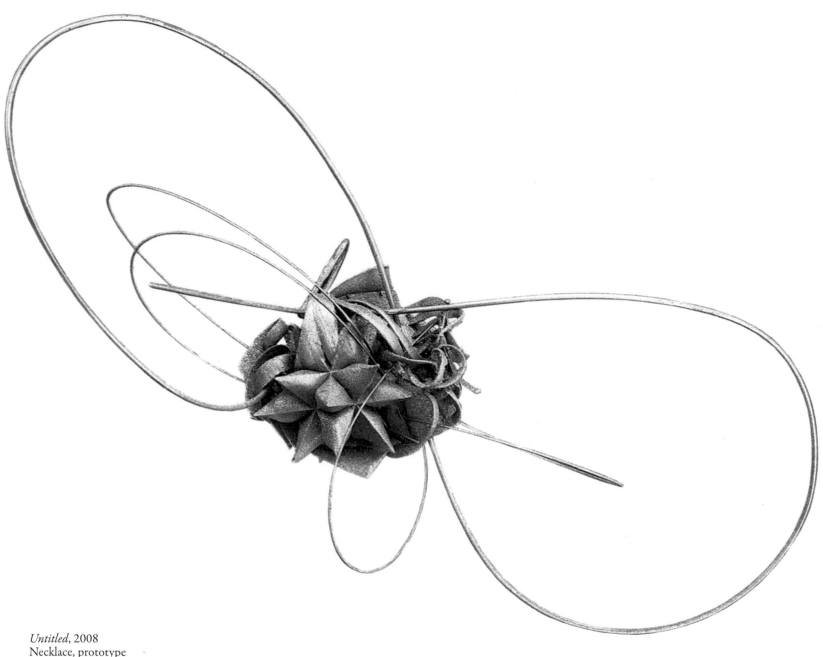

Untitled, 2008
Necklace, prototype
Gold painted on metal, 11" x 1⅞₆ in. (28 x 5 cm)
Unique
Diane Venet collection

Nakis Tastsioglou

Athens 1955–

Nakis Tastsioglou lives and works in Athens. He studied at the Accademia di Belle Arti in Florence from 1975 to 1979. His work uses Plexiglas in combination with iron and light to create primarily geometrical or organic sculptures. He has been involved in many architectural projects, with equal confidence in interior and exterior projects. In the course of a recent visit to the museum in Vergina (Greece), he came up with the idea of a jewelry-sculpture. The resulting Plexiglas necklace engraved with a winged Eros has roots in theology and philosophy. Holding a skull, the god occupies an oval space that refers to the cosmic egg. For the artist, the piece is to be read as a poem on birth, death, rebirth, and the perpetual cycle.

Plex Torque, 2007
Necklace
Plexiglas,
8¹¹⁄₁₆ x 5⅝ x ¾ in.
(22 x 15 x 1.8 cm)
1/7
Diane Venet collection

Sam Taylor-Wood London 1967–

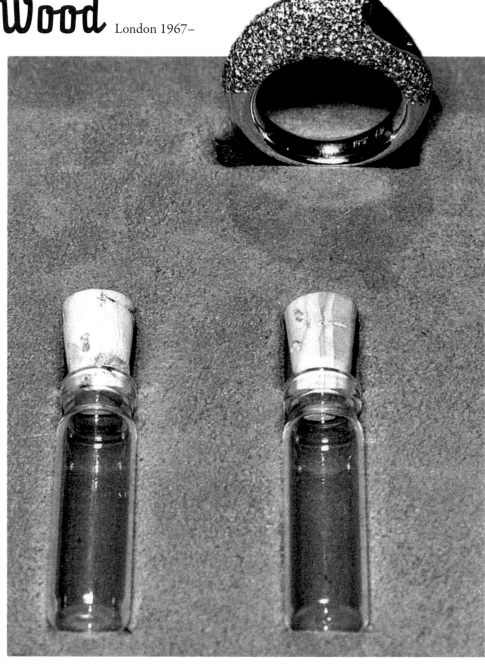

The film-maker and photographer Sam Taylor-Wood likes to examine emotions, displaying them in isolation to represent them more fully. In Crying Men, a series of photographs from 2002, she fixes in black and white images Hollywood film stars crying and leaves us wondering about the expurgated perception that we have of ourselves and of others. Her ironic and subversive language points out enigmatic situations in our society, as we continue to seek perfect and unreal images. For the 2003 exhibition Past and Present at the Louisa Guinness Gallery, Sam Taylor-Wood collaborated with the jewelry designer Shaun Leane to create a piece of jewelry evoking the themes of extreme love and the liberation of feelings. The ring *The Tear Catcher* extracts feelings, happy or sad, which one can then lock into one of five phials with cork stoppers placed in a custom-made leather casket. There are ten copies of this model made in eighteen-carat white gold, set with diamonds. That same year, Sam Taylor-Wood designed the necklace *Cunt* with the word written in bold Gothic script in eighteen-carat white gold, set with rubies or diamonds, each model issued in an edition of ten copies.

Tear Catcher, 2003
Ring
White gold and diamonds, five corked glass vials and bespoke leather box, 1³⁄₁₆ x 1 x ¼ in.
(3 x 2.5 x 0.75 cm) (ring)
Edition of 10, Shaun Leane in collaboration with Louisa Guinness Gallery
Courtesy Louisa Guinness Gallery

Lowell Nesbitt

Baltimore 1933–1993

Further to his meeting with Robert Indiana in 1962, Lowell Nesbitt gave up abstract art in favor of a very personal realistic style, based on the motif of the flower. The artist then specialized in creating brightly colored close-ups of tulips, orchids, and lilies in drawings and very large-scale botanical paintings. He explained his choice in these terms: "I tried to handle the subject of the flower in a monumental way in order to exceed its beauty." Lowell Nesbitt maintained a strong friendship with numerous artists, among whom were Jasper Johns, Andy Warhol, and James Rosenquist, who would all meet at his New York studio. He represented American art on postage stamps, and was also asked by NASA to be the official artist for the space shuttles Apollo 9 and Apollo 13.

The jewelry he produced in the 1970s is marked by the presence of flowers and his use of extremely vivid colors. In 1972, he designed the necklace *Lily* in gold and colored enamel, in association with the editors Gem Montebello. Three years later, it was the natural form of the tulip that he chose to portray in red and orange enamel on a white background, in the shape of a brooch. This ring, produced in an edition of twelve copies, differs from the rest of his production in its use of three different golds, in a composition consisting of four layers of superimposed metals.

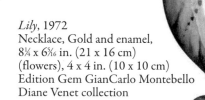

Untitled, 1971
Ring
Three different golds,
height: ⅞ in. (2.25 cm),
diameter: ⅞ in. (2.25 cm)
2/12, edition Gem GianCarlo Montebello
Diane Venet collection

Lily, 1972
Necklace, Gold and enamel,
8¼ x 6⁵⁄₁₆ in. (21 x 16 cm)
(flowers), 4 x 4 in. (10 x 10 cm)
Edition Gem GianCarlo Montebello
Diane Venet collection

146

Corneille

Liège 1922–L'Isle-Adam 2010

Corneille spent his childhood years in Belgium. After a brief stint at the Academy of Fine Arts in Amsterdam, where he found the teaching over-academic, he decided to follow his innate sense of free expression and experiment. After the COBRA movement, which Corneille had cofounded in 1948, dissolved in 1951, he set off to travel the world, visiting Sub-Saharan Africa, Latin America, Mexico, Brazil, Asia, Israel, the United States, etc.

Universally known for his colorful paintings, Corneille is also much admired for the variety of his media. His prints, ceramic sculptures, bronzes, glassware, jewelry, Limoges porcelain crockery, and tapestries, etc. make his multicolored universe available to the greatest number. For more than seventy years, using a personal, vibrant, and enchanting pictorial vocabulary, Corneille combined his chosen forms in an oeuvre that is a paean to unfettered imagination and freedom.

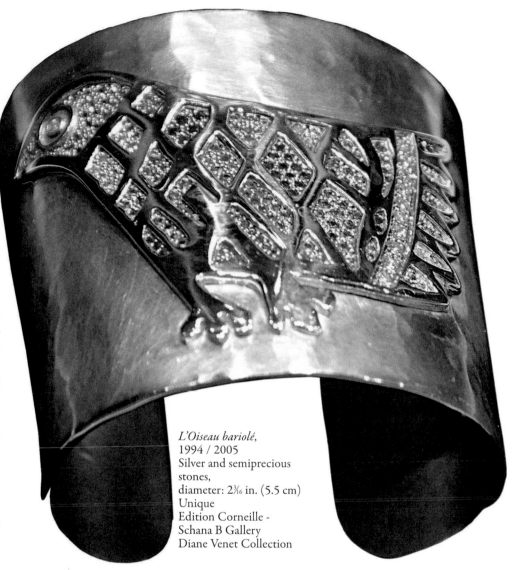

L'Oiseau bariolé,
1994 / 2005
Silver and semiprecious stones,
diameter: 2³⁄₁₆ in. (5.5 cm)
Unique
Edition Corneille -
Schana B Gallery
Diane Venet Collection

Têtes de femmes
Brooch
Silver, 2¾ x 2¹⁰⁄₁₆ in.
(7 x 6.8 cm)
15/99, edition Pierre Hugo
Diane Venet collection

Pop

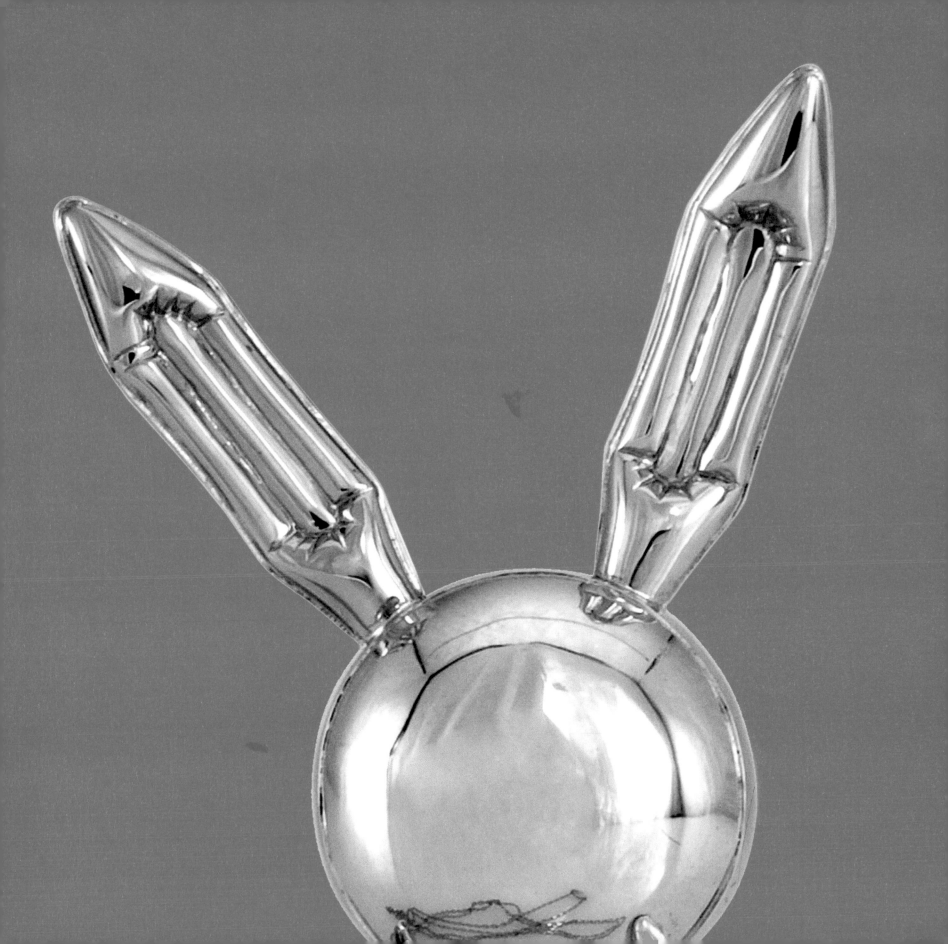

Miguel Chevalier

Mexico City 1959–

A pioneer of virtual and digital art, Miguel Chevalier is a keen explorer of the possibilities offered by new technologies. After a diploma from the École Nationale Supérieure des Arts Décoratifs in Paris in 1983, his broad education and extensive travel enriched his technique. He made his mark on the international scene, in particular in Japan where he was a prize-winner at the Villa Kujoyama in Kyoto in 1994. The digital art of Miguel Chevalier is characterized by countless interactions between the spectator and the work, provoking reflection on the viewer's relationship to the world. The artist manipulates images stemming from cities, from the elements, vegetation, science, and from the history of art in his *Ultra-Nature*, *Flower Fractals*, *Artificial Paradises* and *Flux and Reflux*, allowing them to develop them in time and space to arrive at a synthesis. With their increased digital size and by the amplification of their color, his works force us to look further than is usually possible. Miguel Chevalier has broken down established codes for works of art, creating in 2009 the interactive 3D work *Pixel Snow* for iPhones/iPads, consisting of five snowflakes.

For the realization of a necklace, he returned to the principle of the white bars in aluminum and steel of his *Réseau Fractal Tenségrité* sculpture (2008). Lines cross over to form imbricated phosphorescent squares, a structure that recalls the algorithms or pixels created by his state-of-the-art software. The necklace is thus realized by 3D printer without the intervention of the human hand.

Mini-cubes jaune fluo, 2011
Necklace
Resin, 3D print, length: 39⅜ in. (100 cm)
1/8
Diane Venet collection

150

Michael Craig-Martin

Dublin 1941–

Michael Craig-Martin is widely recognized as an influential art teacher, particularly from his period at Goldsmiths College where he taught many of the future Young British Artists. At the beginning of the 1970s, he became known for his conceptual works. In 1973, he presented the iconic *An Oak Tree*, a glass of water on a shelf, accompanied by a text explaining his intention. The spectator has to look further than the simple objects before him, and must modify his conception of the work, an image questioning the nature of reality. He then worked on paintings using thick black outlines, filled in with bright and matte colors, which he called "nursery colors." Michael Craig-Martin's later work offered a reflection on commonplace objects that he presented on the wall in a variety of different ways: painting, exploration of increases in scale, installations, the projection of 35mm slides. His perpetual questioning on the perception of his work led him to play with the meanings of signs and images.

When making the necklace and earrings *Light Bulb* in 2007, he turned to the motif of the light bulb that had appeared so many times in his paintings.

In 2006, he used it for the neon installation on the facade of Kunsthaus Bregenz and would use it again three years later as the main subject of an acrylic painting on aluminum. These yellow- and white-gold necklaces and earrings were respectively produced in editions from ten to twenty-three copies, and can be compared to his work *Signs of Life* which he created as a universally comprehensive pictorial language.

Light Bulb, 2007, Necklace
White and yellow gold, 1¾ x 10 x 6¼ in.
(4.5 x 25.5 x 16 cm)
Edition of 10,
Louisa Guinness Gallery
Courtesy Louisa
Guinness Gallery

César

Marseille 1921–Paris 1998

jewels that had been desired but were now rejected, by compressing them. They were crushed in such a way that the pieces locked internally and did not require soldering. Loaded with memories of past feelings, they were forever entwined in a solid block worn around the neck. Assembled in the workshops of Gérard Blandin or Pascal Morabito in Nice, then in Paris, each piece was unique. A large number of these compressions remain today simply because of the number of commissions received by the artist.

Among the "microsculptures" invented by César, we also find the compression of capsules, an action inspired by the ironic conception of the management of waste in our consumer society. The "miniaturizations" are another aspect of his work. We find his legendary *Pouce* (Thumb), as well as a reduction of a breast which he had molded on a dancer from the Crazy Horse in Paris.

A student at the Beaux Arts in Marseille, then in Paris, César produced classic sculptures of nudes and animals in scrap metal at the start of his career, then later fired them in bronze. Very quickly he became fascinated by waste and machines, which he appropriated and elevated to the rank of works of art. The "artist-worker" joined the New Realists in 1960, and that same year made his mark at the Salon de Mai by presenting three compressions of cars, assembled by means of a hydraulic press. He did not stop there. After introducing the mechanical world into the artistic sphere, he became interested in the technical properties of polyurethane, the material which allowed him to realize his "expansions," some of which were cast in public, then cut from the block and offered in small, signed pieces.

In the early 1970s, César extended his experimentation to what he called "microsculptures." To create these, he suggested to his friends that he "recycle" their personal jewelry, medals from their childhood, or

Le Sein, c. 1990
Pendant
Gold and diamonds,
diameter: 1%6 in. (4cm)
Natalie Seroussi collection

American Flag Compression,
late 1960s
Pendant
Enameled metal compression,
2½ x ⅞ x ¹¹/₁₆ in.
(6.3 x 2.1 x 1.7 cm)
Unique
Didier Antiques collection

Compression, c. 1980
Pendant
Gold, 2⅜ x 5/8 in. (6 x 1.5 cm)
Unique
Anne de Boismilon collection

.../

…/César

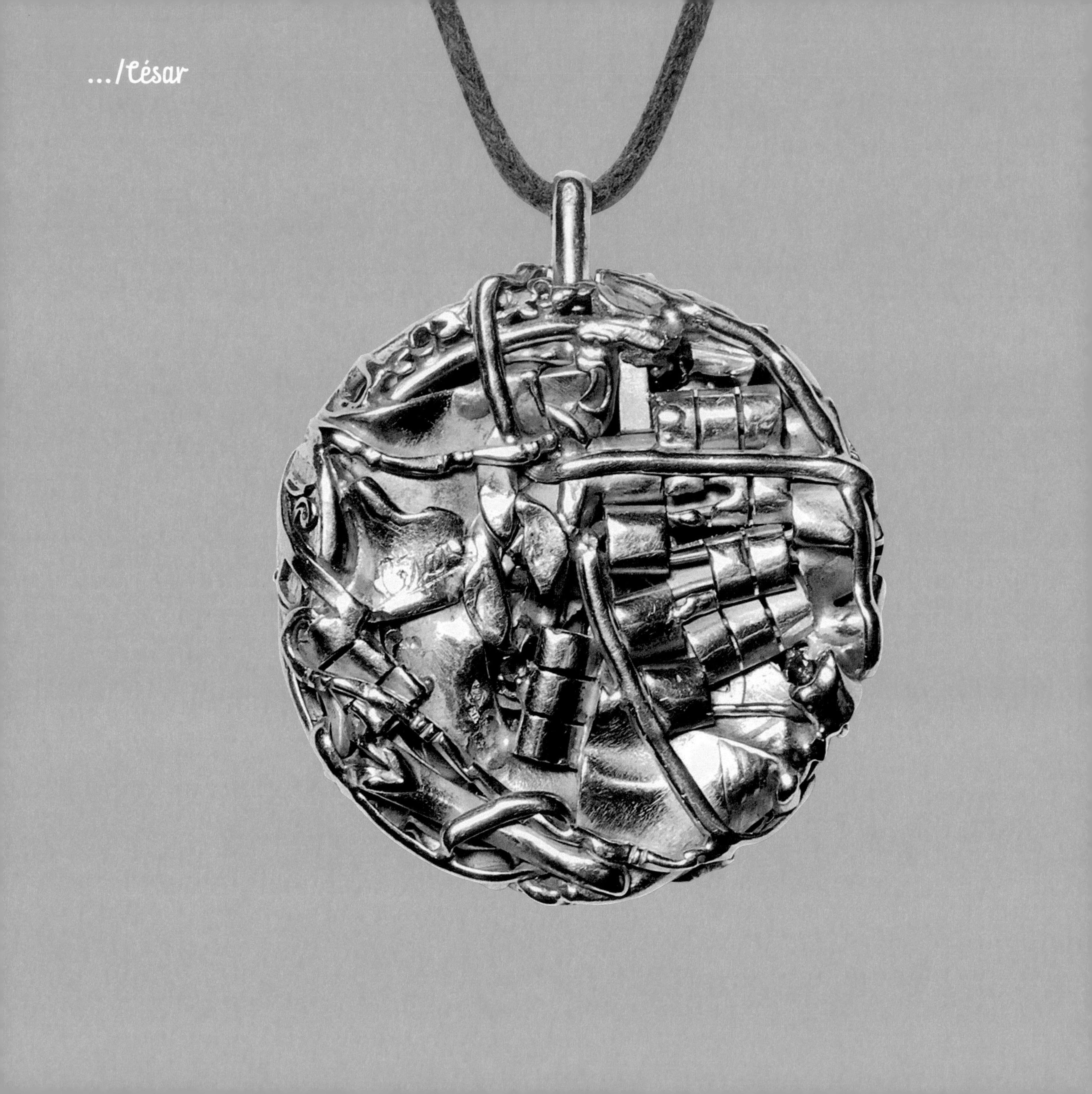

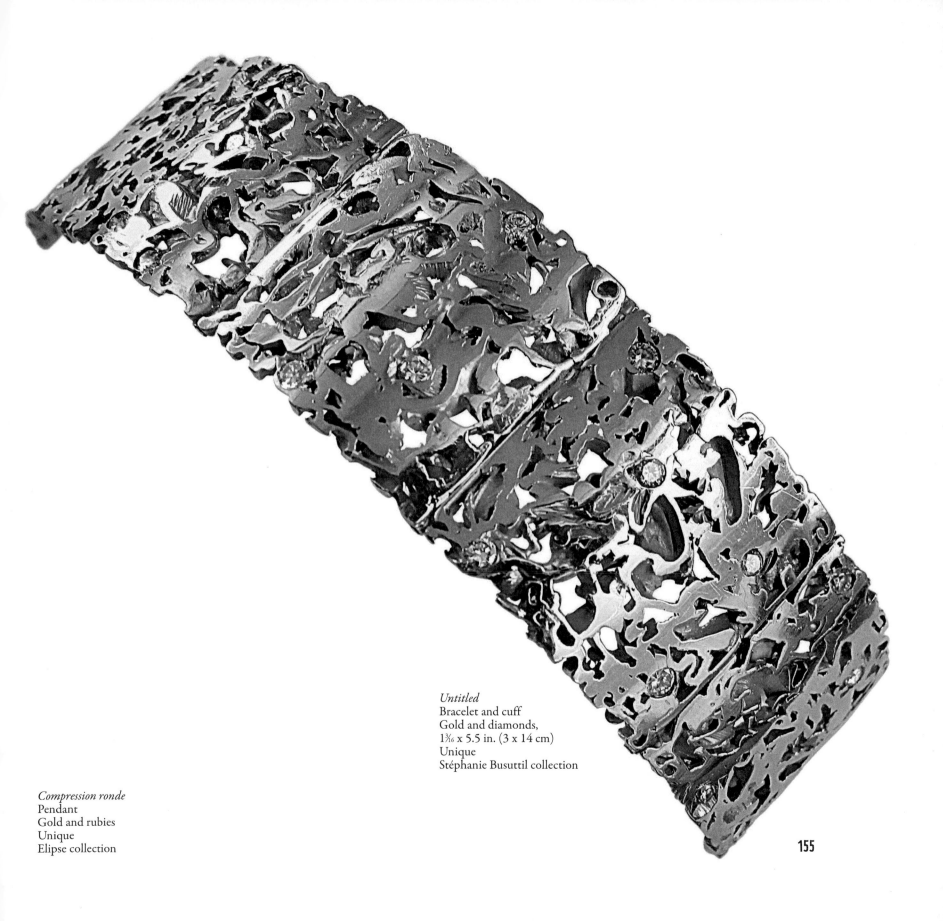

Untitled
Bracelet and cuff
Gold and diamonds,
1³⁄₁₆ x 5.5 in. (3 x 14 cm)
Unique
Stéphanie Busuttil collection

Compression ronde
Pendant
Gold and rubies
Unique
Elipse collection

155

John Chamberlain
Rochester, Indiana 1927–

Since 1957, John Chamberlain has marked the art world with his large, angular sculptures built from discarded elements of automobile bodies that have been compressed and welded. During the 1960s, he integrated into his work other materials such as Plexiglas, brown bags, aluminum foil, galvanized metals, and sprayed automobile paint. He did not try to subject these materials to any prescribed idea, preferring to emphasize spontaneous correlations between the materials. This process terminated in displays of well-worn, rusted, or shiny sculptures. When he used color, it was with a palette full of brilliant tints, mixing turquoise blue with pink and orange. In 1966, he began a totally different series of sculpture tying rolled urethane foam rubber with cord, before becoming interested about ten years later in photography. Influenced by the appropriation of everyday objects in David Smith's work, he began to incorporate metallic tubes, pipes, and iron bars in his deconstructed compositions. His abstract sculptures testify to his interest in the abstract expressionism of Willem de Kooning and Franz Kline, artists he discovered during his studies at the Art Institute of Chicago then at the Black Mountain College, in North Carolina.

John Chamberlain created his first pieces of jewelry in the early 1960s, making several unique models of brooches out of painted aluminum. Their uneven profiles bring to mind the distortions of his large-format sculptures.

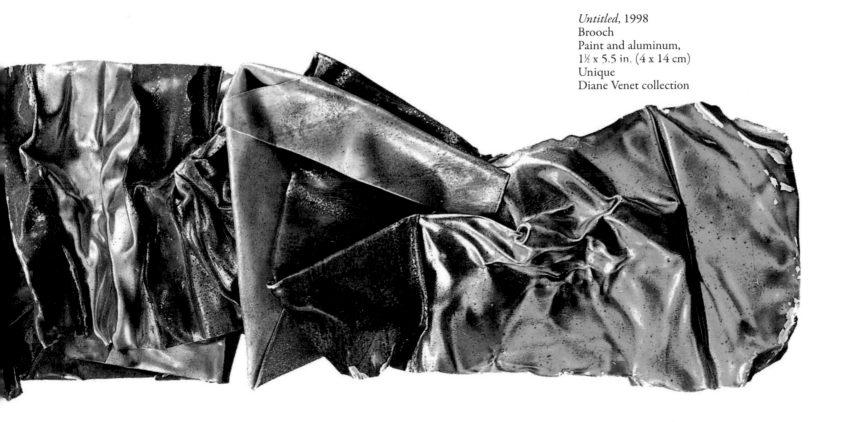

Untitled, 1998
Brooch
Paint and aluminum,
1½ x 5.5 in. (4 x 14 cm)
Unique
Diane Venet collection

Jacques Villeglé Quimper 1926–

Widely considered to be the most influential of all poster artists, Jacques Villeglé defines himself as an "artist-journalist, interested in posters, newspapers, and street art." He has managed his artistic career as if he was not the creator, but a discoverer of his work. The artist embraces urban chaos, hijacking advertising and the press in a subversive way. The posters (which he has collected since 1949) are torn by the passage of time, the weather, or anonymous hands, and according to Villeglé, constitute living works of art, the tracks of civilization. In February 1954, Villeglé and Raymond Hains, who had collaborated since they were students at the Beaux Arts of Rennes, met the Lettrist poet François Dufrêne. It is he who introduced them to the New Realists, a group they joined in 1960.

The jewelry designed by Villeglé refers to his "sociological cryptograms," the modified lettering often found in graffiti done on walls. The ring *Yes*, made in an edition of eight by Patrick Boisgrollier in 2008, recalls his monumental sculpture of the same name created in 2007. These later works show graphics loaded with symbols. The currency sign for the yen, the euro, and the dollar combine assertively to underline the power of ideograms. The bracelet *Star* was made in an edition of eight by Marco Filippini to celebrate the fiftieth anniversary of New Realism. In both cases, Villeglé works with letters, but this time in gold and silver.

Yes, 2008
Ring
Silver, 1¹⁄₁₆ x 1½ in. (2.7 x 3.8 cm)
1/8, edition Patrick Boisgrollier
Diane Venet collection

158

Kenny Scharf Los Angeles 1958–

In the same vein as Keith Haring and Jean-Michel Basquiat, Kenny Scharf is associated with the graffiti that was so ubiquitous in the 1980s. His artistic universe is populated with characters inherited from the cartoons of his childhood, particularly the Flint-stones. He uses this reappropriation of the cartoon to introduce popular culture into the world of fine arts.

His jewelry production is rather recent. He has issued a limited number of pieces using his preferred motifs of hearts, interlaced snakes, stars, "speedy," and the ying/yang symbols reinvented as "ringrang," with child-like, lunar faces. These pieces, which are marketed by Sara Benda's on-line gallery, are realized in eighteen-carat gold, jade, diamonds, enamel, pearls, and sometimes rubies and sapphires. In 2009, he designed a series of six limited editions of watch faces for the Swiss brand of watchmakers Movado, as Andy Warhol had done before him. Very similar to his painted works, we find on these watches the colorful, cartoon-like, playful images familiar from his art.

Speedy, 2007
Necklace
Diamonds, sapphires, pearls, enamel, and painted 18-carat gold, 1³⁄₁₆ x 2¾ in. (3 x 7 cm)
Edition of 50, Afsoun Gallery
Diane Venet collection

Arman

Nice 1928–New York 2005

In its originality and its innovative relationship with the real world, the work of the artist Arman is in harmony with the artistic current of the second half of the twentieth century. At the instigation of art critic Pierre Restany, Arman joined the New Realism movement in 1960, during the first exhibition of the group in Milan. On this occasion, a group of artists: Yves Klein, Jacques de la Villeglé, Jean Tinguely, and Raymond Hains decided to break away from abstraction, the movement that dominated the art scene in the 1950s. For these artists, the object, the image, and the body took on a new meaning and existed as symbols of a world set up as a work of art.

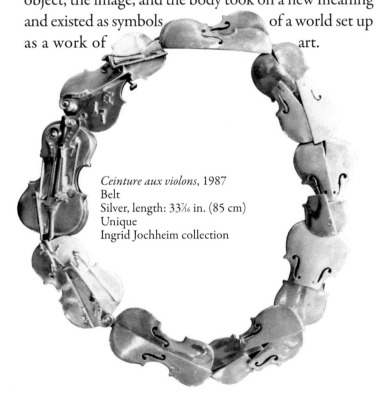

Ceinture aux violons, 1987
Belt
Silver, length: 33⁷⁄₁₆ in. (85 cm)
Unique
Ingrid Jochheim collection

The participation of Arman in this movement was rooted in his own personality, influenced by his childhood as the son of an antiques dealer, as well as his studies at the School of Decorative Arts in Nice and at the École du Louvre. His "accumulations" were a kind of archaeology of the modern world, demonstrating his passion for the objects he collected, objects he often destroyed before bringing them back to life.

The exhibition Empty and Full at the Iris Clert gallery in Paris in 1960 was an accurate reflection of the artist's preoccupations; he filled the gallery space with accumulations of garbage, without, however, losing sight of the aesthetic aspect of the work. He declared in 1989: "I remain a sculptor and a painter whose ambition, before making a speech about ourselves or our civilization, is to produce a work of art."

In the mid-1960s, during an illness which confined him to bed, Arman began making jewelry using elements from watch-making and small, wooden musical instruments. In the 1970s, he started producing editions of his jewelry made in gold and silver in collaboration with several jewelers and craftsmen such as François Hugo, Arthus-Bertrand, Pascal Morabito, Argeco, Artcurial, and Filippini. From these partnerships limited editions were produced, as well as unique pieces closely derived from his artworks. Arman also made multiples in many different mediums to propagate his work to the widest possible audience. The pendants shown here are made of dismembered pieces of a watch, marbles, nails, and violins that have been taken apart then recomposed before being molded in resin and lastly encircled in gold.

Right and following page:
Inclusion, c. 1960s
Pendant
Gold, 1¾ x 1³⁄₁₆ x ³⁄₈ in. (4.5 x 3 x 1 cm)
Unique
Diane Venet collection

.../

Following page, right: *Untitled*, c. 1980
Necklace, Gold, Doris Beyersdorff collection

...../ Arman

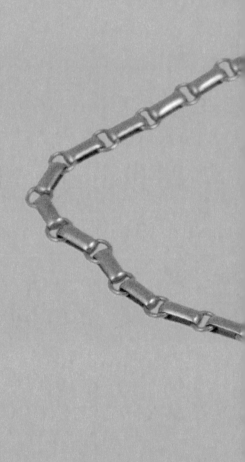

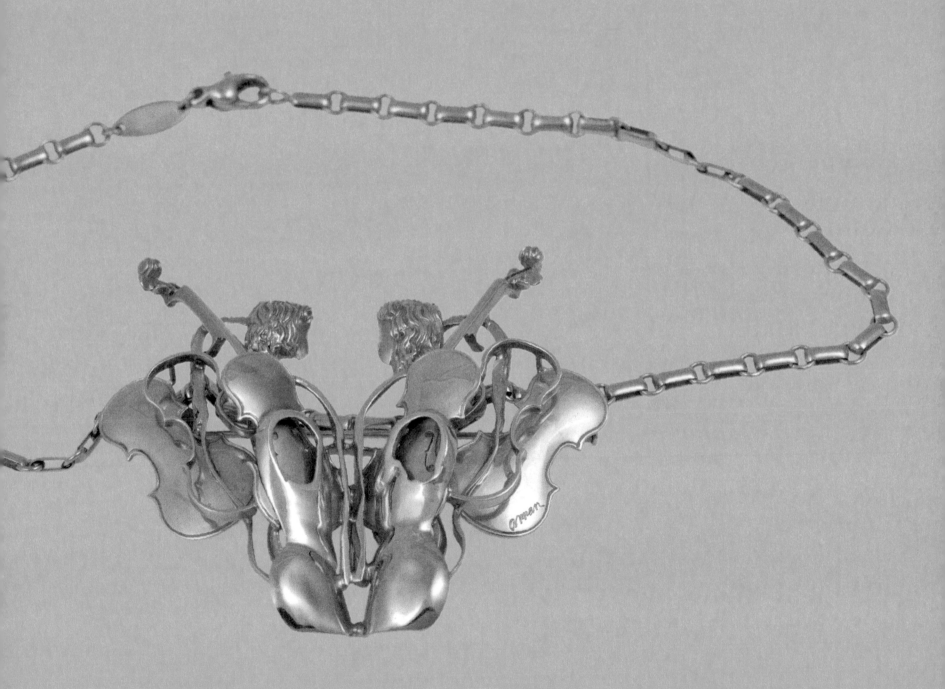

Niki de Saint-Phalle

Neuilly-sur-Seine 1930–San Diego, California 2002

Nana
Brooch
Enamel, 4⁵⁄₁₆ x 2¹⁵⁄₁₆ in. (11 x 7.5 cm)
Edition Gem GianCarlo Montebello
Marina Karella collection

Sculptor, painter, and film director, Niki de Saint Phalle first came to public attention in 1960 with *Tirs* (Shootings), a performance which introduced a new way of painting. The artist fired at pockets of paint which then splattered randomly onto a plaster structure, portraying the violence inherent in every human being. This artistic gesture made an impression on Pierre Restany, who introduced her to the New Realists. In 1965, Niki de Saint Phalle created her first, iconic *Nana* (Young Woman), with her opulent forms, who served to question a woman's role in society. With Jean Tinguely, whom she married in 1971, she created other memorable works, such as the Stravinsky fountain in Paris and the Tarot Garden in Tuscany. Niki de Saint Phalle also made sculptures of snakes, trees of life, women, and lucky charms in the shape of eyes, hands, and four-leaf clovers which she painted in startling, bright colors.

She chose to copy her monumental sculptures in her jewelry-making. With the exception of a snake issued in 1977 by Sven Bolterstein, all of Niki de Saint Phalle's jewelry was created by her friend GianCarlo Montebello. We are struck by the bright colors so dear to the artist, who fashioned jewelry using enamelwork on a base of gold, sometimes set with precious stones.

Visage
Necklace
Enamel and gold, height: 10⅝ in. (27 cm)
Unique
Gem GianCarlo Montebello
Marina Karella collection

.../

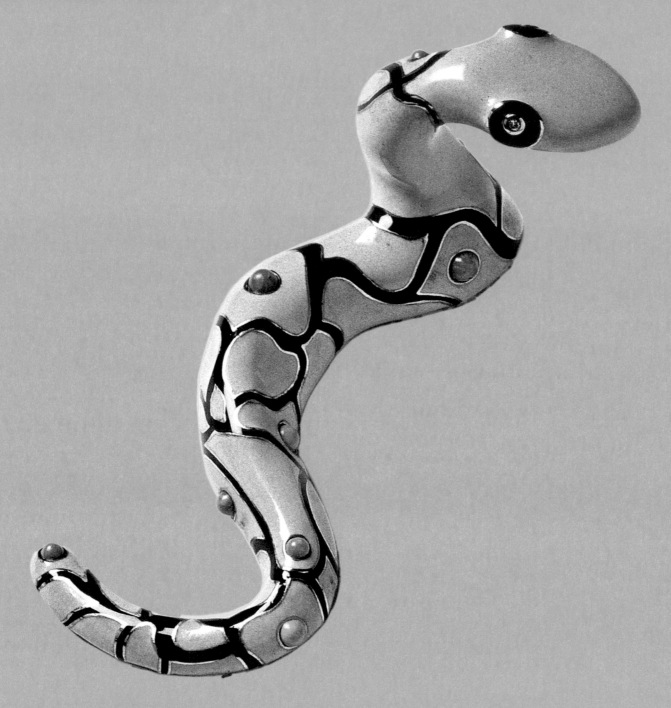

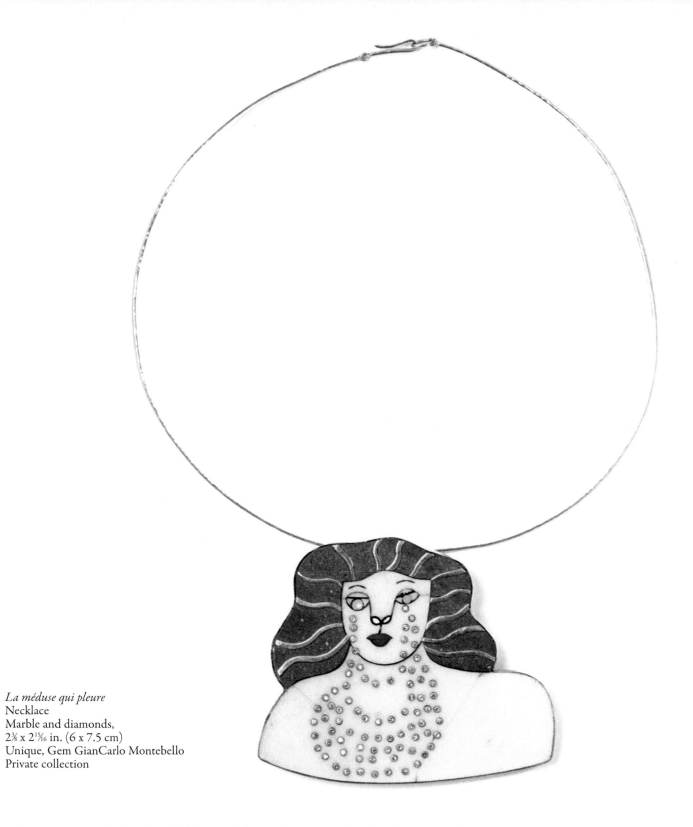

La méduse qui pleure
Necklace
Marble and diamonds,
2⅜ x 2¹⁵⁄₁₆ in. (6 x 7.5 cm)
Unique, Gem GianCarlo Montebello
Private collection

Serpent Jaune, 1977, Brooch / Pendant, Gold, enamel, diamond, turquoise, 3¾ x 1⅜ in. (9.5 x 3.5 cm)
Edition of 8 + 4 AP, Gem GianCarlo Montebello, Diana Küppers collection

Raymond Hains

Saint-Brieuc 1926–Paris 2005

According to gallery owner Iris Clert, Raymond Hains is "king of the metaphysical pun." Before he started manipulating words, the artist ventured into photography from 1947, shooting through distorting fluted glass. This process allowed him to obtain abstract images which ended up as "hypnagogic photographs." After his meeting with Jacques Villeglé at the Beaux Arts in Rennes, Hains began collecting posters torn up by anonymous passers-by. These fragments of papers were presented as they were, or put on a stiff support, as a repository of urban memory. This was the case for the series *La France Dechirée* (France in Shreds), which consisted of political pamphlets referring to the Algerian War. In 1960, Hains met the New Realists and shared with them their ideals of bringing life and art closer together, in spite of, or because of, their differences.

Semantics brought him closer to Lettrism through the influence of the poet François Dufrêne. An erudite man, Raymond Hains also drew inspiration from the writings of Freud, Céline, and Giono.

The *Seita I* brooch refers back to the huge matchbooks presented for the first time by Hains in 1964 at the Italian gallery Del Leone. Conceived as a critique of conceptual art, these matchbooks were presented as being the production of two fictitious artists, Seffa and Seita, representing an Italian and French tobacco company respectively. This model was remade as a piece of jewelry by the artist in 2000 as an edition of eight pieces by Marco Filippini.

Seita I, 2000
Brooch
White and yellow gold,
1¹³⁄₁₆ x 1¹³⁄₁₆ x ¹⁄₁₆ in. (4.3 x 4.3 x 0.2 cm)
3/8, edition Filippini
Diane Venet collection

Robert Indiana

New Castel, Indiana 1928–

With work close to Pop Art, Robert Indiana is thought of as "the American sign painter." Having studied at the Art Institute of Chicago, he settled in New York in 1954. At this time, he used found objects, which he assembled to turn into sculptures. In the 1960s, he chose to use signs, symbols, and familiar and concise words, which he used as strict commands addressed to the spectator. The works *Eat*, *Die*, and *Love* are words set in place in abstract compositions, on smooth and colorful backgrounds. His canvas *Love*, first lettered in 1965, became a universal symbol for the hippie generation. In 1967, Robert Indiana created the *Love* ring, in eighteen-carat gold. Its shape resembles the rings worn by the "bad boys" of the 1950s, whereas the word "Love" refers to a very different state of mind. The artist enjoyed playing with symbols and from 1966 developed work around the word "love" so personal that it became his signature. The graphics of Robert Indiana can be found on monumental sculptures, posters, tapestries, paintings, screen-prints, and even on an American postage stamp.

Love, 1967
Ring
18-carat gold,
1⅛ x 1 x ¾ in. (2.9 x 2.5 x 1.9 cm)
Edition of 8
Bill Katz collection

Andy Warhol

Pittsburgh, Pennsylvania 1928–New York 1987

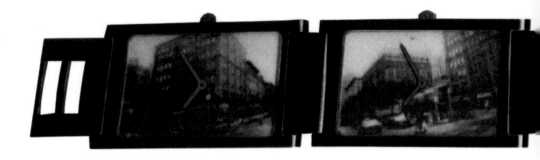

Times 5, 1988
Watch
Dark steel, length: 8⅞ in. (22.5 cm),
diameter: 1 in.(2.4 cm)
225/250, edition Movado
Private collection

170

The son of Czech immigrants, born in the mining city of Pittsburgh, Andy Warhol studied at the Carnegie Institute of Technology from 1945 to 1948. He first achieved fame as a brilliant commercial illustrator before exhibiting and selling his paintings. His two careers of illustrator and artist are closely linked, in terms of both his technique and the themes he chose. Warhol is world famous for his work as a painter, musical producer, author, and avant-garde filmmaker and his ties with diverse social circles including intellectuals, Hollywood celebrities, bohemian eccentrics, and wealthy aristocrats.

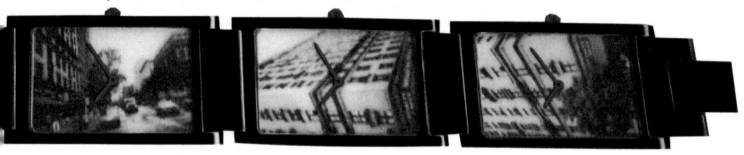

His silkscreen portraits, using one silkscreen print to repeat similar patterns ad infinitum, symbolize the standardization and the cult of the consumer in the new American society of the 1960s.

Just before his death in 1987, Andy Warhol conceived the first artist's watch, in collaboration with the Swiss watch manufacturers Movado. This limited edition of 250 copies was presented at the Basel fair in 1988. The stainless-steel watch consists of five dials representing photographs of New York buildings in black and white, for five different time zones, with red baton hands.

Roy Lichtenstein New York 1923–1997

A quintessential Pop artist, in the 1960s Roy Lichtenstein took inspiration from comic strips and advertizing in trademark works composed of a multitude of small, colored circles painted with stencil and known as *benday dots*. Creating large-size paintings and sculptures whose compositions are actually more complicated than they appear, Roy Lichtenstein accompanied his drawings with ironic texts often critical of American society of his time.

In 1968, the firm Multiples Inc. of New York published a pendant brooch created by Roy Lichtenstein. This piece, entitled *Modern Head*, was issued in two versions: the first deploys the kind of primary color palette frequently employed in his Pop works, while the second was produced in black and white monochrome. The pieces were unveiled at the exhibition, "Jewelry to Sculpture to Jewelry," in Boston in 1973. As for the *Teardrop* pendant, it reuses the tear and profile of the blonde who appears in the one of his canvasses, *Crying Girl*.

Modern Head, 1968
Brooch
Enamel on metal, 3 x 2¼ in.
(7.8 x 5.8 cm)
Edition Multiples, Inc.
Collection Rosalind Jacobs

Pendant, 1965
Cloisonné
Enamel on metal
3 1/2 x 2 1/2 inches
8.9 x 6.4 cm
Edition of 6
Lichtenstein Foundation

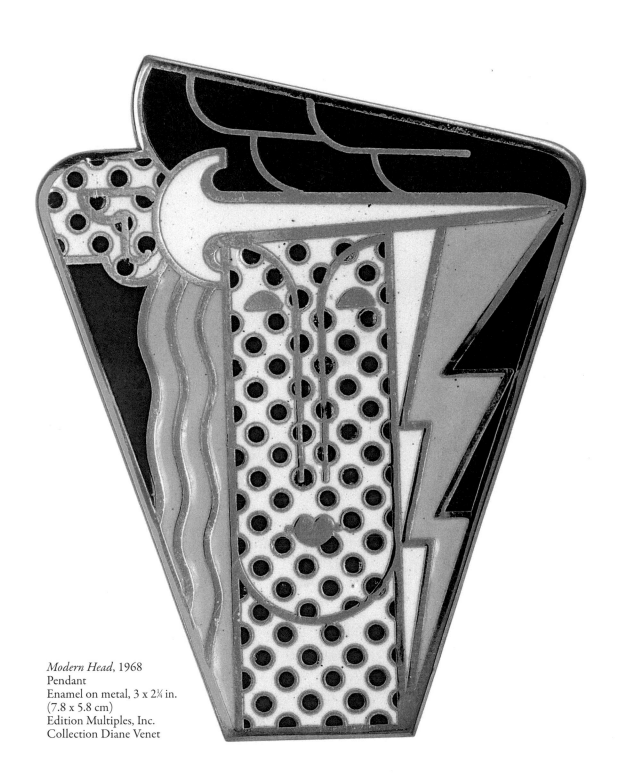

Modern Head, 1968
Pendant
Enamel on metal, 3 x 2¼ in.
(7.8 x 5.8 cm)
Edition Multiples, Inc.
Collection Diane Venet

Dinos Chapman

Cheltenham 1962–

A member of the "Young British Artists," Dinos Chapman studied in London at the Royal College of Art. In the 1990s, having for a time acted as assistant to the artists Gilbert & George, Dinos started making collaborative works with his brother, Jake.

Turning to sculpture, they used resin figurines to set up elaborate scenes concerned chiefly with torture. Deliberately provocative, the two artists have become past masters in the art of controversy.

The violent iconography they create explodes in works peopled by mutant children (*Fucking Faces*, 1994), decomposing skulls (*Sex I*, 2003), or ghostly figurines redolent of the Holocaust (*Hell*, 2000). Great admirers of Goya, they rehearse the Spanish master's engravings in horrific compositions whose chief themes are sex, war, and capitalism.

In creating a jewelry model for gallery-owner Louisa Guinness, Dinos centered his research on a type of nut that can be tightened around the neck or wrist, constraining it. The necklace *Wingnut and Bold Choker* and the bracelet *Jubilee Clip* in silver were issued in one hundred copies.

Wingnut and Bolt Choker, Jubilee Clip, 2010
Choker and bracelet with chain and key
Silver, choker diameter: 4¾ in. (12 cm) (adjustable),
bracelet diameter: 2⅜ in. (6cm) (adjustable)
Choker: 12/100, bracelet: 2/100,
edition Louisa Guinness Gallery
Diane Venet collection

174

Kader Attia Dugny 1970–

Kader Attia mixes different genres and confronts different cultures and convictions, calling on our subconscious to reveal its deeply buried fears. A Frenchman of Algerian origin, this artist is enveloped in various traditions: Moslem, Jewish, and Christian. This cultural melting pot, seen through the contemporary eye of the artist, are the basis of his inspiration. Kader Attia uses various media (video, photographs, installations) to create intentionally provocative works.

The ring *Menottes* (Handcuffs) that he created in white gold in 2007 is a unique piece; it joins two fingers together. Kader Attia had already used this idea in 2006, in his installation *Moucharabieh* in which overlapping handcuffs formed the repeated motif for the architecture of a Moorish window, a kind of grill which allows us to see through without being seen.

Menottes, 2007
Ring
White gold, 1 x 3¹³⁄₁₆ in. (2.6 x 9.7 cm)
Unique, edition Jean-Jacques de la Verrières
Diane Venet collection

Peter Klasen

Lübeck 1935–

Co-founder of the New Figuration movement in 1962, Peter Klasen's work consists
of presenting a personal language full of contrasts. He associates smooth material with
rough objects, the techniques of airbrush
and collage, the theme of weapons to that
of the woman.... These contradictions assert
themselves in his fragmentations of the
human body or machines which he brings
out in both his paintings and photography.
A believer in the power of art to transform
society, Peter Klasen fights against the divi-
sions established by an "art for art's sake."
His production of jewelry takes place in the
continuation of his research on limitation
and the ambiguity of technological progress.
The composition of the silver necklace he
made in 2006 recalls his *Tableaux-Rencon-
tres* of the 1960s by the effect it produces on
the body. Flashes of lightning strike the bust
from the neck, creating an atmosphere
loaded with meaning, similar to those paintings where he cuts up images and then
reassembles them in a way without any
apparent connection.

Untitled, 2006
Necklace
Silver,
6⁵⁄₁₆ x 1⁵⁄₁₆ in.
(16 x 5 cm)
Unique
Marie Haddou collection

176

Keith Haring

Reading, Pennsylvania 1958–New York 1990

Keith Haring's synthetic figures surrounded by a black line or simply drawn in chalk were an iconic feature of American urban spaces—in the subway, on sidewalks, or outside warehouses—in the 1980s. Often right under the nose of the authorities, he drew hearts, barking dogs, or other active characters. His lines were inspired by graffiti and usually decorated in vivid colors. These easily understandable images often dealt with sensitive subjects of the day, such as apartheid or AIDS.

Influenced by Andy Warhol, he made use of the American consumer society to make his works known to a wide public, and in 1986 opened his Pop Shop in the district of Soho, New York. Music inspired him, in particular hip-hop, and he collaborated with numerous singers such as David Bowie, Grace Jones, and Madonna.

Keith Haring's jewelry recalls the recurring themes of his work. They were widely reproduced in eighteen-carat gold and some are covered with enamel. The model of the *Radiant Baby* is his most well-known image, symbolizing life, energy, enjoyment, and hope.

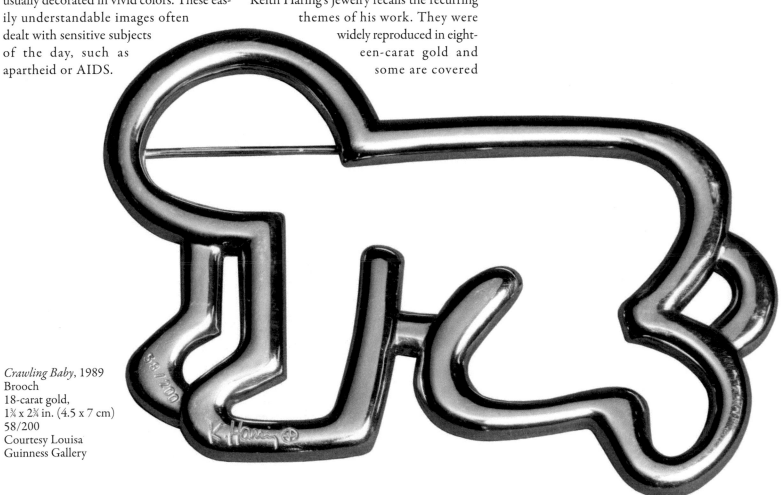

Crawling Baby, 1989
Brooch
18-carat gold,
1¾ x 2¾ in. (4.5 x 7 cm)
58/200
Courtesy Louisa
Guinness Gallery

Karel Appel
Amsterdam 1921–Zurich 2006

The first works of Karel Appel were marked by the very brief influence of Picasso, Matisse, and then Dubuffet. Having participated in the artistic experiments of the Dutch Experimental Group in Amsterdam, Appel joined the international CoBrA (an acronym of Copenhagen, Brussels, and Amsterdam) movement in 1948, founding with his friends Corneille, Constant, Asger Jorn, Noiret, Jan Nieuwenhuys, and Christian Dotremont a different artistic conception, in contradiction with the fashionable abstraction of the time. Settling in Paris in 1950, Karel Appel tried to keep a lively spontaneity in his paintings, later making reliefs in plywood, layering vivid colors applied to themes of figures, portraits, landscapes, and nudes. For this artist, nothing was more important than to see the child in the man, and it is for this reason that he was inspired by the spirit of children's drawings in compositions which he later refined. The theme of the cat is also recurring in the work of Karel Appel. He came back to it in 1975 for the brooch *Madam and her Cat*. Made of gold and acrylic on resin, it reflects the boldness of line and the solid colors that characterize much of his work.

Madame et son chat, 1975
Brooch
Gold, resin, and acrylic,
2³⁄₁₆ x 2¾ in. (5.5 x 7 cm)
AP 2/8
Diana Küppers collection

Enrico Baj

Milan 1924–Vergiate 2003

Throughout his life as an artist, Enrico Baj continued to develop his critical, even satirical ideas about post-war society. Influenced by his studies of medicine, law, then art at the Accademia di Brera in Milan, he invented a whole universe populated with caricatural characters in the 1950s. Generals bedecked with medals, old ladies adorned with braids, everything was a pretext to denounce the bourgeoisie and the military system. An anarchist, he co-founded with Sergio Dangelo the movement Arte Nucleare in 1951, declaring their opposition to the threat of a nuclear war. Very politically active, Enrico Baj signed numerous texts about art, and in 1954 joined Alechinsky, Jorn, and Appel to launch the Mouvement International pour un Bauhaus Imaginiste, before establishing the magazine *Il Gesto* the following year.

In the 1970s, he started making jewelry and designed brooches and pendants in silver, gold, and enamel in which can be seen synthetic forms of the figures found in his collages or scored into thick coats of paint. The artist worked with the jewelers Unoaerre, who used industrial techniques in their artistic work with metals. They collaborated with several artists, such as Salvador Dalí, whose jewels can be seen in their museum collection.

Untitled, c. 1970
Pendants (4 small parts, one piece)
Enamel on sterling silver, 2¼ x 1¹³⁄₁₆ in. (5.7 x 4.6 cm)
362/400
Martine & Didier Haspeslagh, Didier Antiques collection

Pol Bury

Haine-Saint-Pierre 1922–Paris 2005

Firstly influenced by surrealism and the group CoBrA, of which he was member from 1949 to 1951, the Belgian artist Pol Bury became involved with another artistic universe in 1950. That year, he visited the exhibition dedicated to Alexander Calder at the Maeght Gallery. It impressed him so much that he abandoned painting in favor of sculpture from 1953. He focused his research on the aesthetic movement of slowness. Ionesco spoke of a "philosophy of slowness" to redefine his work. Pol Bury used geometrical forms in such diverse materials as wood, stainless steel, or polished copper. He then added an electric motor that provoked an imperceptible movement in the sculpture. He became one of the main proponents of kinetic art, and by the end of the 1960s he was also devoting himself to writing, and to the realization of fountains and jewelry.

The latter are created from cardboard models which the artist had produced at different times by Gem Montebello, F&F. Gennari, Artcurial, and the jeweler Jacques Bugin for the Maeght Gallery. Extensions of his other works, the jewelry is often an exact replica of a sculpture in a reduced dimension, made of gold or silver. This time it is the body which creates, by its movement, the mobility of the elements.

Untitled
Bracelet
Gold
Edition Gem GianCarlo Montebello
Diane Venet collection

Mimmo Rotella

Catanzaro 1918–Milan 2006

After his studies at the Accademia di Bella Arti of Naples in the 1950s, Mimmo Rotella produced paintings close to geometrical abstraction. In search of a new artistic approach, in 1953 he tore up his first poster, ripping it from the wall and slashing it again in his studio. In 1958, he met the critic Pierre Restany, thanks to whom he joined the New Realists three years later. The works of Mimmo Rotella are nevertheless different from those of his French peers Hains and Villeglé because he acts directly on their surface, rejecting the process of anonymous laceration. The work of Rotella is very close to previous movements, such as dadaism, as witnessed by his production of various ready-mades such as the sculpture *Small Monument to Rotella*, a tin of oil on which the Shell logo is relabeled with Rotella's name. After his installation in Paris in the 1960s, he came to fame for his series Spectacles-vérités and his appropriation of film images, often of an erotic nature. In 1975, he made a record from his phonetic musical poems named *Epistaltism*, a kind of "laceration of words," or repetition of blurred sounds. From 1980, he returned to painting, particularly using acrylic, to create his "overpaintings," collages that he then reworked. In 1993, he created a brooch named *Torn up Poster*, a unique piece that made direct reference to his earlier work. The artist tore up a poster which he signed, then placed inside a small silver frame mounted as a brooch. In 1998, Mimmo Rotella collaborated with Editions Filippini, producing a series of eight gold pendants with the motif of a tortoise.

Untitled
Cigarette case
Silver gilt,
5¹⁵⁄₁₆ x 2¹⁵⁄₁₆ in.
(15 x 7.5 cm)
Diane Venet collection

Yves Klein Nice 1928–Paris 1962

Yves Klein's work needs to be understood in the context of his practice and teaching of judo and the mysticism of the Rosicrucians. In 1956, when he created IKB (International Klein Blue), the philosophical thinking of the artist became explicit: "Blue has no dimension, [...] All colors bring forth associations of concrete, material and tangible ideas, whereas blue evokes even more the sea and sky, which is what is most abstract in tangible and visible nature."

This metaphysical search for immateriality in his work led the artist to perform *Le saut dans le vide* (Leap into the Void) in 1960. Like the *Anthropometries* and the *Cosmogonies*, it also evoked themes of the exterior and passage. Using women's naked bodies covered with ultramarine blue paint as living paintbrushes, or even the wind and rain to bring their strength to his work, the artist is channeling an idea: that is enough for him. The brooch-pendant *Petite Vénus bleue* (Small Blue Venus), an edition of five hundred, is characteristic of Klein's work, and would be instantly recognizable even without the signature. The bronze statuette is covered with blue IKB, and floats inside a Plexiglas box lined with gold leaf, both colors that Klein uses for his monochromes: the blue symbolizing space, and the gilt the sacred. From its shape, it could be mistaken for one of the *Anthropometries*, while its structure echoes his famous portrait of Arman, a plaster cast painted in IKB, also lined with gold leaf. Its title is a reminder of one of the last creations of the artist made just before his final, fatal heart attack. It is the readymade Venus, a torso that Klein covers once again in his patented blue, to express his refusal of the academic standards inherited from the Renaissance, and his appropriation of a "dematerialized" world.

Petite vénus bleue, c. 1960
Brooch
Brass and spray paint,
2⅜ x 1 in. (6 x 2.4 cm)
Atelier Jean-Paul Ledeur
Diana Küppers collection

183

Günther Uecker

Wendorf 1930–

Both a painter and sculptor, German artist Günther Uecker has used the nail as the centerpiece of his work since the mid-1950s. He creates works close to kinetics, using such varied media as paint and household objects. Metallic tubes are fixed to his work to create an interaction of light and shade. Through Yves Klein, his brother in-law, Günther Uecker met Otto Piene and Heinz Mack, who had founded the group Zero, and in 1961 Uecker joined this group. At this time, he developed his exploration into light, time, and space, and added to it a reflection on politics and human suffering. Little by

little, he abandoned figurative art, starting to work in design and also directing movies. These changes encouraged him to sporadically use new materials such as water and sand, but using a hammer and nail remains at the heart of the majority of his works.
In 2011 he created a ring on which the gold protrusions seem nailed onto their base. Produced in association with the editors Gem Montebello, it is reminiscent in shape of his *Chair with Nails* (2007).

Untitled, 2011
Ring
Gold, 1³⁄₁₆ x 1⅜ x 1¾
(3 x 3.5 x 4.5 cm)
1/8, Gem GianCarlo Montebello
Diane Venet collection

Jeff Koons

York, Pennsylvania 1955–

The conceptual and popular approach of Jeff Koons caused a stir in the art world of the second half of the twentieth century and has led to his work being exhibited in many private and public collections around the world, from the Château of Versailles to François Pinault's collection.

In 1985 this former commodities broker at the Wall Street stock exchange displayed toys in Plexiglas boxes at the New Museum of Contemporary Art of New York. In 1980, he created the series The New, comprising everyday household appliances exposed in illuminated Plexiglas display cases. In 1986, with the series Statuary, he attacked the recurring symbols of artistic iconography. Gradually, Koons developed his mercantile and pornographic installations, becoming the master of kitsch through his use of improper objects, such as his famous *Rabbit*, an inflatable rabbit made of stainless steel with a mirror surface.

His works are unusual in that they are realized in media as different as wood, stainless steel, glass, and marble, and are fabricated by up to one hundred assistants in his workshop situated in Chelsea, New York.

In 2005 Jeff Koons reappropriated the symbolic figure of the rabbit in his production of fifty white-gold pendants for Stella McCartney with the Sonnabend Gallery. He also scaled down the sculpture for her 2006 runway show in Paris, an event which the artist and the fashion designer prepared in close collaboration.

Rabbit Necklace,
2005–09
Pendant
Platinum,
Height: 2¹⁵⁄₁₆ in. (7.5 cm)
11/50, edition Jeff Koons
for Stella McCartney
Diane Venet collection

185

Yayoi Kusama Matsumoto 1929–

Untitled
Necklace
Wool, 11¹³⁄₁₆ x 5⅛ in. (30 x 13 cm)
Unique
Diane Venet collection

In the 1950s, the Japanese artist Yayoi Kusama began to produce drawings and watercolors using repetitive motifs derived from the hallucinations she suffered in her childhood. She moved on to an exploration of male domination in art and more particularly Pop Art, by means of installations and performances. In 1962, she created *Accumulation No. 1*, a work which introduced her usage of soft phallic protrusions. She has used the phallic shape in most of her work since that time, including on furniture and utilitarian objects, covering their surfaces. To this is added a plethora of colored dots, her preferred motif. In the 1970s, she orchestrated a series of happenings concerning the antiwar movement and nudity. After a stay of about fifteen years in the United States, she decided to return to live in Japan in 1973. Feelings of depression led her in 1977 to elect to live permanently in a psychiatric hospital; she continues to create in a studio nearby. Recently, Yayoi Kusama designed cases for Japanese cell phones, expanding her pictorial universe beyond the artistic sphere. The same applies to her jewelry, such as the necklace created from small balls of wool.

187

Grayson Perry

Chelmsford 1960–

Doll Pendant, 2008
Necklace
6 ¹¹/₁₆ x 6 x ⅝ in.
(17 x 15.25 x 1.5 cm)
Edition of 5,
Louis Guinness Gallery
Diane Venet collection

Grayson Perry became known on the international scene for his ceramic vases, but he has also worked in other media such as textiles, embroidery, cast iron, lithography, and photography. His movies and performances in the 1980s, at a time when he was a member of the Neo-Naturist Group, were slowly overtaken by his work as a potter, in which he uses autobiographical images of himself. Another important part of his life is as a transvestite called Claire. To embody the personage of Claire, he disguises and adorns himself with outrageous dresses and wigs, often dressing just like a child's doll. He may hide behind a colorful and provocative mask, but this does not prevent him from integrating into his work a genuine critical reflection on our society, and its politics and consumerism. The images he puts forward are often charged with references to violence, art history, and to sex, by means of complex techniques and materials rarely used in the fine art world because of their similarity to handicrafts. Grayson Perry respects the traditional forms of these arts, but transforms them with his palette full of colors and the gravity of the subjects he chooses.

In 2005, he made a first incursion into the world of jewelry, evoking the power of lucky charms. The winner of the 2003 Turner Prize realized a sculpture in the shape of a hare for *God Please Keep my Children Safe*, imagined as a Victorian amulet and presented at the exhibition Love is at the National Gallery. In 2007, he collaborated with five other celebrities in the realization of a necklace for the benefit of cancer research. His participation in this project consisted of designing one of the suspended charms in the shape of a miniature ceramic vase, a favored motif. That same year he created a reliquary pendant for the Tate Modern of London. In 2009, he collaborated on the jewelry collection The Cherry on the Cake initiated by the Victoria and Albert Museum of London. The institution asked several artists and designers to design a piece of jewelry to be issued in limited numbers. He used textiles, a material that he had already worked with, and created colored figurines, faithful to the outfits and postures of his alter ego Claire.

Tatsuo Miyajima
Tokyo 1957–

Installation artist and sculptor Tatsuo Miyajima graduated from the Tokyo National University of Fine Arts and Music in 1986. Since 1988, he has staged numerous projections of numbers by means of light-emitting diodes and LED-counters. For this artist—whose three fundamental principles are perpetual change, the relationship with other people, and infinite continuity—the numbers he uses in his work convey a language comprehensible to all, free of cultural connotations. These three elements are also fundamental to Buddhist culture. He often works with new materials such as electric wires, stainless steel, or metal mirrors, but retains a spiritual approach toward his work. The series Diamond in You (2010) makes reference to the notion of *kongochi*, the highest form of enlightenment in Buddhism and also to the purest diamond present inside

every human being, the one which will bring wisdom to him.

His first counters, from 1988, did not register zero, and his rings follow the same principle. Each ring is endowed with a counter going from 1 to 9 or from 9 to 1. This particularity of never reaching absolute nullity (already seen in his series Region), allows the artist to represent a symbolic universe where death is absent. The speed of the counter on the rings goes from 0.1 to 299.9 seconds according the wishes of the owner. In 2009, Tatsuo Miyajima created the *Times Ring* in an edition of ten copies, in association with the Elisabetta Cipriani Gallery. It consists of a series of three rings of which the composition differs: the first one is in pink gold, containing a green LED

screen; the second one is in white gold with a screen in white LED; and the third ring in yellow gold has a screen in blue LED.

Time Ring, 2009, Ring, 18-carat red gold with green LED, 18-carat white gold with white LED, 18-carat yellow gold with blue LED and 2 batteries, 1¹¹⁄₁₆ x 1½ x 1½ in. (4.3 x 3.9 x 3.9 cm), Edition of 10, Elisabetta Cipriani, Elisabetta Cipriani collection

Meret Oppenheim

Berlin 1913–Basle 1985

Painter, poet, and creator of objects, Meret Oppenheim was a major figure in the surrealist movement. Besides her own personal work, she was a model for the photographer Man Ray, with whom she exhibited at the Salon of Surindependants in 1932. It was Alberto Giacometti who inspired her first surrealist sculpture: a small bronze named *The Ear of Giacometti*.

The artist liked to change the original usage of everyday objects, giving them a parallel new meaning. By this process of misappropriation, she created *Lunch in Fur*, a cup, saucer, and spoon completely covered in fur. The work was such a success that it was snapped up by MoMA.

The artist revisited the idea in 1935, but this time it was a metal bracelet which she surrounded in fur. Meret Oppenheim did not stop there, and invented many other surrealist pieces of jewelry such as a necklace made of small bones arranged in parallel lines.

The gold and onyx ring is one of her more recent creations from around 1984.

Untitled, 1984–86
Ring
Yellow gold and onyx,
diameter: 1⅜ in. (3.5 cm)
Edition of 10, Cleto Munari
Diane Venet collection

190

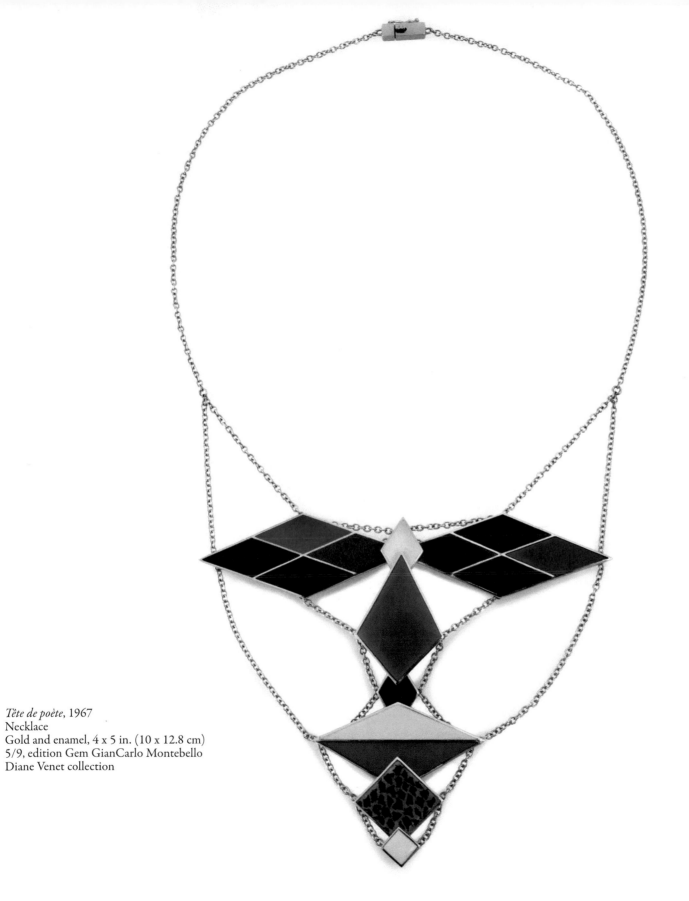

Tête de poète, 1967
Necklace
Gold and enamel, 4 x 5 in. (10 x 12.8 cm)
5/9, edition Gem GianCarlo Montebello
Diane Venet collection

191

Jack Youngerman

Saint Louis, Missouri 1926–

Youngerman's first works, created in the mid-1940s in Paris, where he studied at the École des Beaux Arts, are marked by their abstract geometry. At this time, his work was inspired by Henri Matisse, and Jean Arp and constructivism. On his return to the United States in 1956, he started to explore variations of colors, illusions capable of modifying optical effects. He was interested in the organic form relating to living things, which he reinvented by means of a lively and brilliant color palette. In the 1950s he was interested in the tactile properties of his work, covering his canvases with a thick coat of paint, but he changed his technique from the 1960s, adopting acrylic for a smooth, slick finish, allowing him to reinvent shapes with sharper outlines as he produced bigger and bigger paintings. In 1970, he created a series of works by means of cut canvases, then produced his first sculptures and painted reliefs.

In 1969 Youngerman started a collaboration with the editors Multiples Inc. which led to the creation of a pendant-brooch made of silver metal and blue and white enamel; it was shown at an exhibition in Boston in 1973. The central motif is inspired by a flower represented by contrasting solid blocks of color.

Untitled, 1969
Brooch / Pendant
Enamel and silver, 2¾ x 2 in.
(7 x 5 cm)
Edition Multiples, Inc.
Barbara Rose collection

Yoko Ono

Tokyo 1933–

Plastic artist, singer, musician, writer, and experimental film-maker, Yoko Ono created her first artistic works at the beginning of the 1960s, influenced in this by the musician and minimalist artist John Cage whom she met in 1958. Soon after, she joined the group Fluxus and unleashed her imagination and performances onto the public. In 1965, she presented at Carnegie Hall in New York her conceptual happening *Cut Piece*, undoubtedly her most famous artistic activity. Seated on the floor in a traditional Japanese posture, she allowed spectators, equipped with extraordinarily large scissors, to cut fragments off her clothing until she was completely naked, expressing in a theatrical way human suffering.

In 2004 she created, in association with the editors Filippini, two pieces of jewelry, both in eighteen-carat white and yellow gold in an edition of eight copies. The ring *Imagine Peace* reminds us of Yoko Ono and John Lennon's multiple artistic actions in aid of peace, actions which led to their being recognized worldwide as symbols of the peace movement of the 1970s. The title refers to the well-loved song *Imagine*, and is also the name, chosen by Yoko Ono in 2007, for the disk-shaped tower that was erected in Iceland to pay tribute to John Lennon, on what would have been his seventieth birthday.

The pendant *Make A Wish When the Sun Hits* echoes her numerous *Wish* installations and performances presented from the 1990s. In 1991, one of her works simply instructed visitors to make a wish when the sun hits, hence the title of the pendant.

Imagine Peace, 2004
Ring
White and yellow gold,
1½ x 1½ x 1½ in.
(3.75 x 4 x 4 cm)
8/8, edition Filippini
Diane Venet collection

Nam June Paik

Seoul 1932–Miami, Florida 2006

Nam June Paik, a member of the group Fluxus, marked the history of art by his performances and installations developed on television screens. A music composer, he broadened the field of visual arts by means of numerous collaborations, in particular with the cellist Charlotte Moorman whom he asked to play the score on a cello made of video monitors, topless, for his *Opera Sextronique* (1967). Nam June Paik carried out an in-depth artistic exploration of technological products, including video. Strongly influenced by the work of John Cage, he created a very personal iconography by a process of "recycling" television screens, connected to the society in which he lived. And so developed *The Family of Robots*, where he used out-dated electronic machines to represent the older members of the family, and the very latest technologies for the younger ones.

When it came to creating a jewel, he dug into his artistic repertory and invented a unique model for a pendant. It consists of a wide pectoral made up of parts of an electronic circuit, realized in metal and resin.

Untitled, 1980
Pendant
Metal, resin, 2¹⁵⁄₁₆ x 2³⁄₁₆ in.
(7.5 x 5.5 cm)
Unique
Natalie Seroussi collection

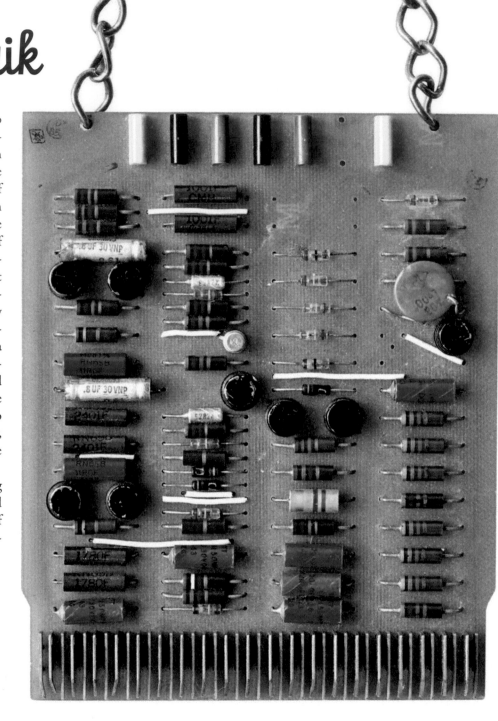

194

Arne Quinze Ghent 1971–

Belgian designer and sculptor Arne Quinze is renowned for his *Cityscapes*, painted, monumental, futuristic installations constructed using painted wooden planks, situated in public places. The instigator of many different projects, the artist is also the creator of everyday objects such as shoes, interior designs, and even furniture, as epitomized by the creation of the very uncomplicated Primary Pouf in 1999. He collaborates with prestigious brands such as Swarovski and Louis Vuitton, is artistic director for the singer Lenny Kravitz, and also manages a studio of sixty people that produces his works based on dreams and freedom. He has also instigated various powerful artistic acts such as the cremation of his sculpture *Uchronia* during the Burning Man festival in Nevada in 2006.

For Arne Quinze, in art "borders are there to be crossed." And this is what he proved in 2010, with his first incursion into the world of adornment. Making a unique piece of jewelry for the head called *My Safe View*, he showed that by using his materials of preference, namely wood painted red and electrical wires, he is able to transpose his originality into a different sphere.

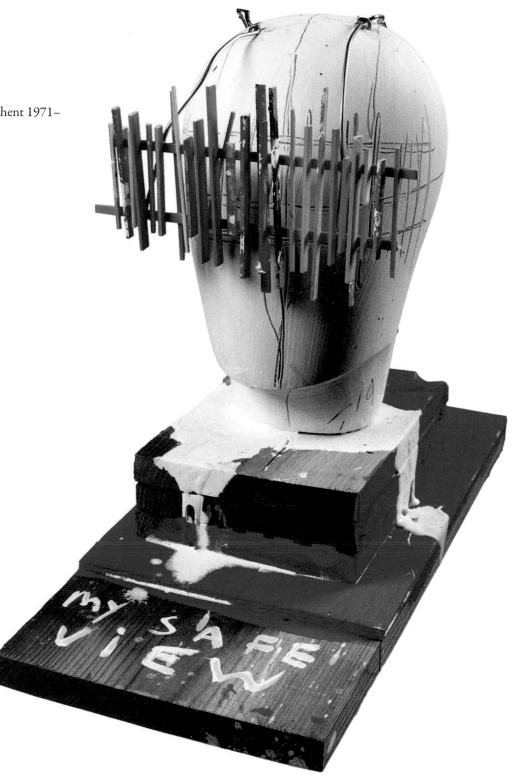

My Safe View, 2010
Headpiece
Wood, paint, electric wire,
13¾ x 7½ x 16½ in.
(35 x 19 x 42 cm)
Unique
Arne Quinze collection

195

Robert Rauschenberg

Port Arthur 1925–Captive Island 2008

In tune with Marcel Duchamp's innovative ideas, Robert Rauschenberg proposed a conception of art which would not exclude any material or natural aspect within his field of exploration. In 1955, when he created his famous painting *Bed*, the artist used his own real sheets attached to a traditional vertical support incorporated into the painting, and launched his series Combines. Generally he would try, through his artistic approach, to take his place as an artist: "Painting relates to both art and life [...] (I try to act in that gap between the two.)" This vision proved to be influential, particularly as it was taken up by the practitioners of Pop Art. Robert Rauschenberg created numerous engravings, collages, installations, and happenings in collaboration with artists such as John Cage, Merce Cunningham, and David Tudor. His works from this time include modern notions of music, dance and photography; around 1962, he became interested in recycling.

When he ventured into jewelry-making in 1990, he employed industrial materials to create a brooch, using discarded objects attached with metal rivets. This unique piece brought a fresh eye to the issue of the recycling of materials in a consumer society, and so to the process of artistic reinvention. The abandoned, everyday object became ornament.

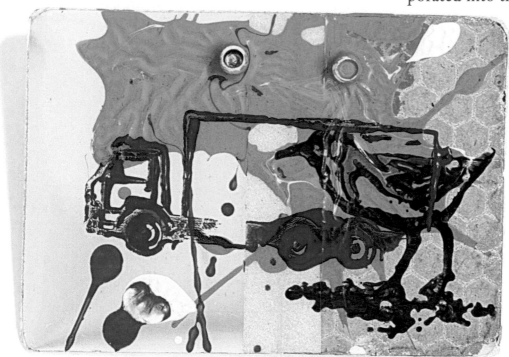

Untitled, 1990
Brooch
Mixed materials, 1¹⁵⁄₁₆ x 2¼ in. (5 x 7 cm)
Unique
Diane Venet collection

Untitled, c. 1990
Brooch
Diane Venet Collection

Donald Sultan

Asheville, North Carolina 1951–

Sultan's first works were representations of objects reduced to simple geometric forms: cut-out and filled-in white tables, a cigarette, a pistol. From 1983 onward, still-life took a more prominent place in his work with weighty but flat images that used more vivid colors: numerous fruits, oranges, apples, or a series of flowers in vases, such as groups of big black tulips. All his subjects are set against very different, stark backgrounds of oil-cloth, masonite, linoleum, even dead leaves treated with latex or tar spread with a knife or a blow torch. These somber paintings are mostly inspired by the chaos of our industrial society, derailments, fires, as seen in newspaper photographs. Sultan's complex technique plays with the contrasts of light and shade.

In 2008, Donald Sultan designed the necklace *New York Survival*, made up of cigarettes and matches. The motif of the cigarette is recurrent in his work. He used it notably in his 1980s' painting *Cigarette*, and again in 1997 for a gouache on paper entitled *Three Cigarettes*.

New York Survival, 2008
Necklace
Cigarettes and matches,
diameter: 13 in. (33 cm),
cigarette length: 3¼ in. (8.3 cm)
Donald Sultan collection

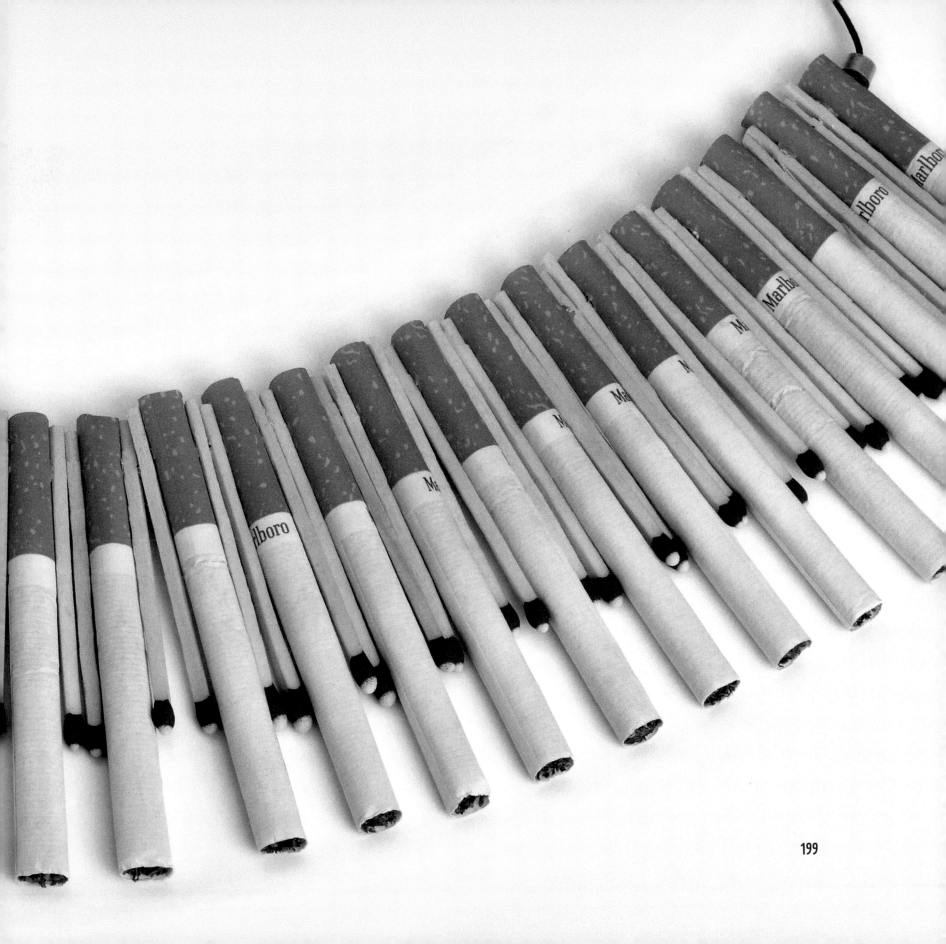

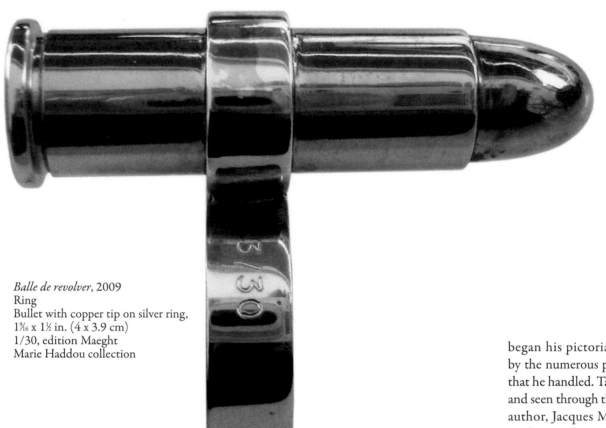

Balle de revolver, 2009
Ring
Bullet with copper tip on silver ring,
1⁹⁄₁₆ x 1½ in. (4 x 3.9 cm)
1/30, edition Maeght
Marie Haddou collection

Jacques Monory Paris 1924–

One of the first members of the new narrative figuration movement, Jacques Monory rejected the abstract, geometrical, and conceptual art in fashion in the 1960s. His specific interest was a hyperrealist approach to subjects dealing with society, and using photographic reproduction, treated his work in mainly monochrome blue, yellow, or pink. Trained as both a graphic designer and a decorator, he occupied the post of art director at the publishers Editions Delpire for ten years. It was at this time that he began his pictorial work, partly inspired by the numerous photographic documents that he handled. Taken from the real world, and seen through the subjective eyes of their author, Jacques Monory's series of works exploit violence, death, and the notion of time by appealing to our buried fears. Whether in his series Roman-photo (2006–8), his book-objects (from 1975), or his video performances, he knew how to create an immediately recognizable atmosphere using subtle nuances of color, light, and shade.

In correlation with his series Murders (1968), and the heavy atmosphere of his paintings, Jacques Monory created in 2009 the ring *Bullet*. It consists of the cartridge of a .38-caliber bullet in brass with a copper tip, set in a solid silver ring and produced in an edition of thirty copies.

Jean-Jacques Lebel Paris 1936–

"I'm seventy-three years old and I don't give a fuck. On foot, on horseback, or in a sputnik." Dropped into an interview given to the magazine *Article XI*, this sentence summarizes quite well the state of mind of Jean-Jacques Lebel. Since the 1960s his paintings, installations, happenings, videos, and writings have skillfully mixed art with politics. His criticisms of certain social phenomena over the years were influenced by his faithful adherence to the principles and ideals of May 1968. A forerunner, he was the first person to present a happening in Europe: *L'Enterrement de la Chose* (The Burial of the Thing) in Venice, where he put a shroud on a Jean Tinguely sculpture before sliding it into the canal during a grandiose funeral ceremony. It was a tribute to a murdered friend, and represented a serious criticism of the violence present in society. After this, he became an active member of several groups, in particular that of the surrealists. Close to Duchamp and to Dadaist ideas, Jean-Jacques Lebel enjoyed being involved in collective works. In 1979, he created the international festival of poetry Polyphonix, which brought together numerous artists, poets, musicians, and video directors to work together on common projects.

Always provocative, Jean-Jacques Lebel designed for the collector Diane Venet in 2010 a particularly suggestive necklace constituted of coins, American cents, with crowned heads mixed with hollow rifle cartridges. In the same vein, he produced in the 1990s a pair of earrings for the collector Clo Fleiss in which he boldly combined gold, amethyst, and teeth.

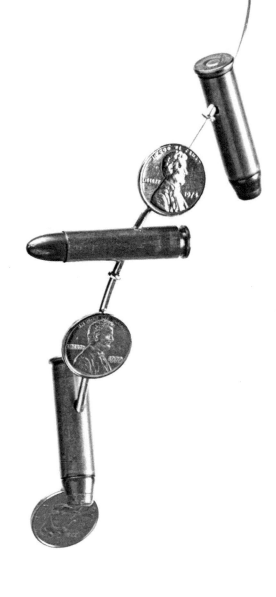

Le Collier de l'arène, 2010
Necklace
Bullets, american cents
and euro cents
Bronze and copper,
7¹⁄₁₆ in. (18 cm)
Unique
Diane Venet collection

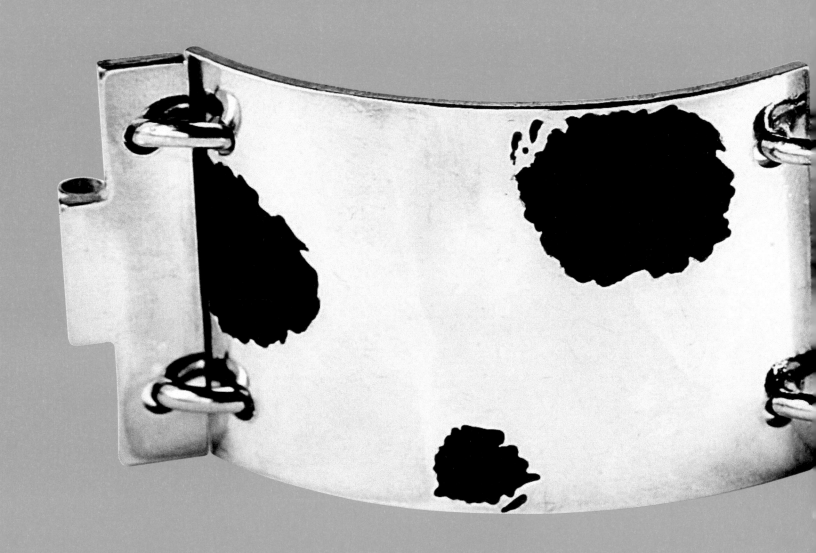

minimalists

Lucio Fontana

Rosario 1899–Comabbio 1968

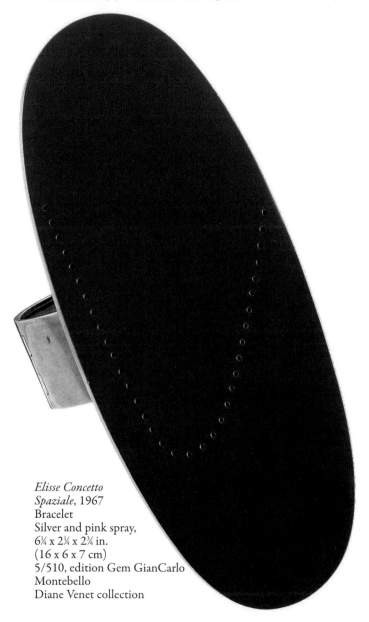

Elisse Concetto Spaziale, 1967
Bracelet
Silver and pink spray,
6¼ x 2¼ x 2¾ in.
(16 x 6 x 7 cm)
5/510, edition Gem GianCarlo
Montebello
Diane Venet collection

The founder of spatialism, with artists such as Gian-Carlo Carozzi, Roberto Crippa, and Cesare Peverelli, Lucio Fontana used flat, bright colors for his paintings, made bronze sculptures, and would later pierce the surfaces of his works. During his youth, Fontana went back and forth between the sculpture studio of his Argentinean artist father and Milan, where he studied sculpting at the Accademia di Brera. In the 1930s, his work was influenced by expressionism and abstraction, even joining the group Abstraction-Création in 1935. During this period he used bronze and ceramic in his sculpture, with strong, expressionistic effects. It was in 1945, at the time he started his exploration of spatial concepts, that his artistic style came into its own. His desire to break with traditional forms of art encouraged him to invent his own personal style of expression. He created "buchi" (holes) and "tagli" (slashes), in his series of *Concetto spaziali* (Spatial Concepts). With their lacerations, the works became a representation of space, time, and infinity. From this time, for Lucio Fontana, "the painting is not or is no longer a support, but an illusion."

His jewelry harks back to the spatialist principles. From the 1950s onward he created some unique pieces in the studio of the Pomodoro brothers, cutting and piercing holes in the surface of the gold, and using the name *Concetto spaziale* once again. In the 1960s, he designed a second series of jewels, this time in association with the editors Gem Montebello. He made five different sets of jewelry, of silver lacquered in various colors, in an edition of one hundred copies.

Following pages:
Left: *Concetto Spaziale*, c. 1950, Brooch, Gold, 1½ x 1¼ in. (4 x 3.2 cm), Unique, Louisa Guinness collection
Right: *Elisse Concetto Spaziale*, 1967, Bracelet, Silver and white spray, 6¼ x 2¼ x 6¾ in. (16 x 6 x 17 cm)

10/150, edition Gem GianCarlo Montebello, Courtesy Louisa Guinness Gallery

Facing page:
Concetto Spaziale, c. 1950
Brooch, Gold,
2¼ x 1½ in. (5.5 x 4 cm)
Unique
Diane Venet collection

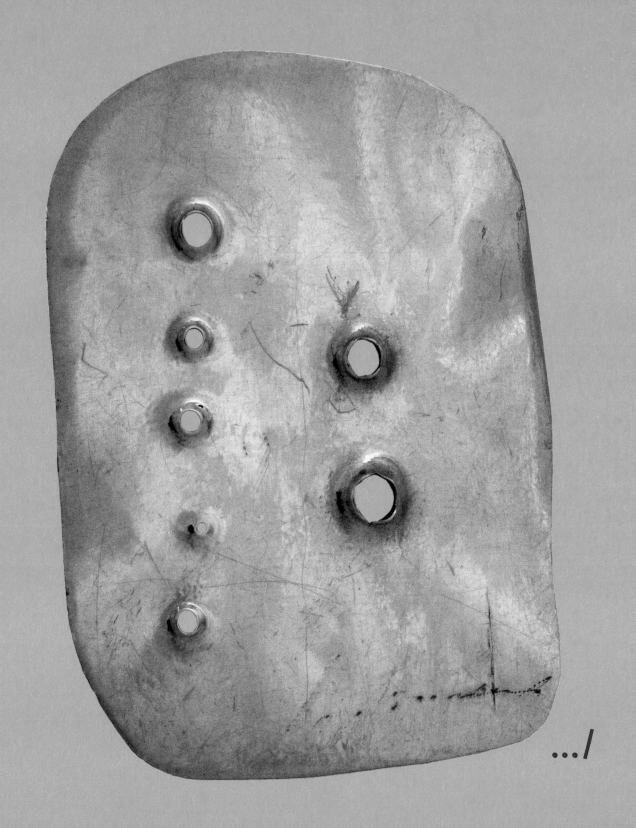

...l

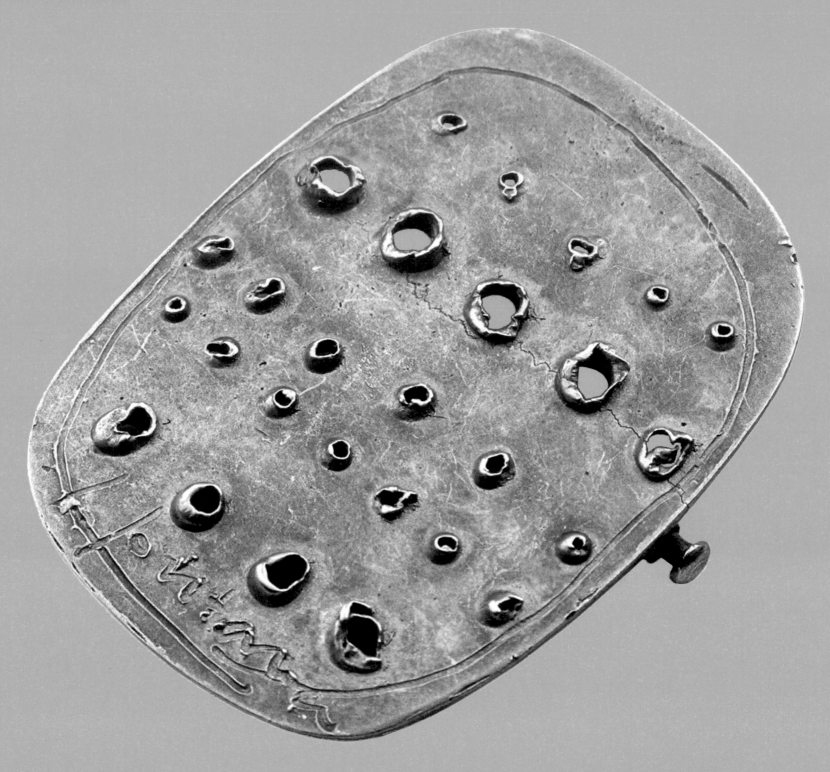

Pierrette Bloch Paris 1928–

"Painting is all about the secret, with what is secret even to oneself." And so Pierrette Bloch defined her vision of art. The secret of the dots that fill most of her work is connected to the rhythm of movement, a sort of personal handwriting for the artist. She develops these motifs mostly using black ink. They repeat themselves and roam through the sheets of paper, and when it is not dots or loops, it is her *Sculptures de Crin* (Sculptures in Horsehair), made by aligning rough knots of horsehair on nylon thread. She makes free with the settings of her works, imposing her vision of space and time on them in a kind of repetitive and infinite promenade. If her technical means seem poor at first sight, it is however beyond a doubt that Pierrette Bloch, who was a friend of Pierre Soulages, Henri Goetz, and André Lhote, has come up with an innovative artistic vocabulary. She also collaborated with the carpet-manufacturing companies Gobelins, de Beauvais, and de la Savonnerie. She created an articulated bracelet, made in silver by the jeweler Patrick Boisgrollier. On this piece we can see the recurring motif of dots that she used in her first paintings, their movement livening up the surface with their rhythm.

James Brown

Los Angeles 1951–

Close to primitivism and the work of his friend Basquiat, James Brown's early works evoke ancient masks, Asian funerary urns, or found objects stuck on a background of linen. In his paintings, he presents shapes using a primitive imagery, his crude drawing with washed-out outlines and collage creating a subtle game of appearance and disappearance. Defined by a vision of nature, the work of James Brown leans toward the dissolution of organic forms, with sources ranging from the literary to the scientific. The artist, who studied at the École des Beaux Arts of Paris in the 1980s, decided to settle in Mexico, where he mostly lives and works at present.

In 1991, he created ten cuff bracelets and seventeen brooches in association with the editors Fremont and the American silversmith Allan Adler. Together, they produced jewelry using a solid base in silver, which as in some of the works painted by the artist, is destabilized by the coral color and the delicacy of the pearl which decorates it.

Untitled, 1991, Cuff bracelets, Silver, coral, 3¾ x 2¾ in. (9.5 x 7 cm)
7/10, edition Vincent Fremont, James Brown collection

BB 5, 2008
Pendant
18-carat gold, 7½ x 4⅛ in. (19 x 10.5 cm)
Unique, edition Francisco Pancheco
Grassy collection

Anthony Caro New Malden 1924–

According to the American art critic Clement Greenberg, Anthony Caro puts "the accent on the pictorial qualities of sculpture, and its ability to draw in space." Influenced by the work of Henry Moore, whose assistant he was from 1951 until 1953, then by the geometric, steel sculptures of David Smith, Anthony Caro turned to modernism in the 1960s, before inspiring a whole generation of artists as a teacher at Saint Martin's School of Art. His sculptures are characterized by an assemblage of steel plates, pipes, beams, and mesh welded or bolted together. These industrial, recycled objects are then painted a bright, flat color, quite altering their appearance. In a break with traditional sculpture, Caro eliminated the base from his works, allowing the spectator to approach and interact with them from all sides. It was an exhibition at the Whitechapel Gallery, London, in 1963, that propelled him onto the international art scene. From the 1980s, he reintroduced more literal elements into his work, such as figures from ancient Greece.

His production of jewelry came rather late. The idea took form in 2003, during the preparation of an exhi-

BB 1, 2008
Pendant
Silver, 2 x 5¼ in. (5 x 13.4 cm)
Unique, edition Francisco Pancheco
Diane Venet collection

bition where the artist envisaged a change of scale in his work. He collaborated with the jewelers Grassy in Madrid to create a series of unique pieces in gold and silver, similar to his monumental sculptures. There are many parallels between productions: the earrings *BB 14* borrow the linear movement from his sculpture *Emma Dipper* (1977), and the ring *BB 16* is inspired by the composition of his yellow steel work *Midday* (1960).

Sol LeWitt

Hartford 1928–New York 2007

A former graphic artist in the office of architect Ieoh Ming Pei, Sol LeWitt's first sculptures were strongly marked by the principles of the Bauhaus and De Stijl. In the 1960s he became a conceptual artist, using mathematical principles to apply as many modifications as possible to geometrical forms. The square, the rectangle, and the line were his preferred figures, which he adapted to form sculptures and wall drawings. He worked using such precise guidelines that he could entrust the realization of his creations to his assistants.

212

For him, only the idea counted, the execution was secondary. He typified American art of the 1960s—along with Carl André, Donald Judd, and Dan Flavin—by introducing innovative ideas in sculpture.

In 2000 he created two rings intended for his daughters. The title *Lines in Four Directions* evokes his minimalist work; he has used the simple motif of bands of engraved lines in the gold and silver. We find the same process of a grid of lines in the *Wall Drawing no. 273 (7th wall)*, executed in 1975.

Lines In Four Directions, 2000
Rings
18-carat gold and silver, 2½ x 7½ in.
(6.3 x 19 cm)
Unique
Collection Sofia LeWitt

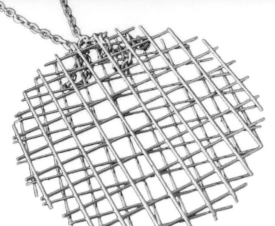

Trame Disques quadrillés argentés, 1967
Diameter: 2³⁄₁₆ in. (5.5 cm)
Diane Venet collection

Cercle inscrit dans le carré, 1978
Necklace
Stainless steel, 2¾ x 2¾ in. (7 x 7 cm)
Collection Danielle Morellet

François Morellet
Cholet 1926–

François Morellet began his working life in the 1940s at his father's side in the family firm, later becoming a self-taught artist. After a brief flirtation with figurative painting, he turned toward geometric abstraction at the beginning of the 1950s. Like Piet Mondrian, he used simple shapes, assembled lines, and restrained colors, which he separated or layered together according to a precise plan. In 1961, he joined the Group of Research into Visual Art (GRAV), and realized a series of kinetic works. In 1963, this developed into an interest in neon tube lighting, so dear to the minimalists. Some time later, he created monumental works that explored the relationship between space and architecture and inspired him to make even more constrained geometrical forms. The titles of his works are important for their understanding, given the artist's belief that a work of art refers to nothing but itself. So the necklaces he made in stainless steel in 1978—*The Diagonal of the Square* and *Circle Inscribed Within the Square* participate in a mathematical construction of his art. The chrome-plated pendant made of two identical cross-hatched disks created in 1967 shows the importance of the overlapping lines, as in his *Trames* (Mesh) of the 1960s. At the beginning of the 1980s, François Morellet made a necklace in Plexiglas issued in an edition of eighty-five copies for the Society of Friends of the Museum of Modern Art of the City of Paris.

214

Anish Kapoor

Mumbai 1954–

From the early 1980s, Anish Kapoor has integrated into his sculptures a reflection on shape and subject. He uses mainly concave and convex forms in his sober sculptures, which play with shadow and light. Anish Kapoor represented Great Britain at the Bienniale in Venice in 1990, and was awarded the Premio Duemila prize there, before obtaining the Turner Prize in 1991. The relationship of man to his environment is an essential feature of his work and has led to him collaborating on an increasing number of architectural projects. One of his sculptures from the Sky Mirror series, which he unveiled in 2001, has been reflecting alternately the sky and the bustle of the Rockefeller Center in New York since 2006. It is a device of contrast and imagination; its concave mirror involves both the spectator and his environment as the constituent parts.

In 2003, at the request of gallery owner and collector Louisa Guinness, he produced a limited edition of twenty-two-carat gold rings. His jewelry unquestionably evokes his monumental sculptures. A gold base is hollowed out in the center, leaving a space which seems intended for a precious stone, but which is left empty, giving the illusion that it contains a drop of water. In 2010, he collaborated with the jewelry-makers Bulgari for whom he designed the *B.ZERO1* ring in a pure, concave shape.

Water Ring, 2003
Ring
22-carat gold and blue enamel,
diameter: 1⁹⁄₁₆ x 1⅜ in. (4 x 3.5 cm)
Edition of 10, Louisa Guinness Gallery
Courtesy Louisa Guinness

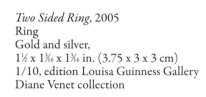

Two Sided Ring, 2005
Ring
Gold and silver,
1½ x 1³⁄₁₆ x 1³⁄₁₆ in. (3.75 x 3 x 3 cm)
1/10, edition Louisa Guinness Gallery
Diane Venet collection

Jaume Plensa Barcelona 1955–

Jaume Plensa uses materials as diverse as bronze, wrought iron, alabaster, resin, salvaged materials, and water in his compositions, which fluctuate between figurative and abstract art depending on the stages of their creation. His works are given a poetic dimension by their appropriation of light, which he often associates with the use of cast iron. The words and the letters incorporated into his works also empower his creations with a spiritual depth. His anthropomorphic sculptures realized on a human scale evoke deep emotion, stimulate intellectual engagement, and also represent a metaphor for the soul. As well as creating sculptures, Jaume Plensa also works on drawings and collages, and has designed some preparatory layouts for carpets to be produced at the French National Manufacturers in Beauvais. His drawings, often in black and white, are sometimes illuminated with light colored touches or with collages, which bring to mind his more sculptural works.

The model for a necklace that Jaume Plensa created in an edition of seven copies is a miniature reproduction of his installation *Jerusalem* (2006), reusing the motif of a gold circle. With the original sculpture, the spectator was invited to hammer on the eighteen monumental gongs by means of a mallet, inviting a reflection on sounds and silence in a purposefully confined space. The necklace, due to its positioning on the body, recalls this initial function. And Plensa also adds a philosophic reflection to the work by engraving in the center of the disk the sentence: "One thought fills infinity."

One Thought Fills Immensity, 2010
Necklace
Diameter: 3⁹⁄₁₆ in. (9 cm)
2/7, edition Stamped P & 750
Courtesy Christian Scheffel Gallery
Private collection

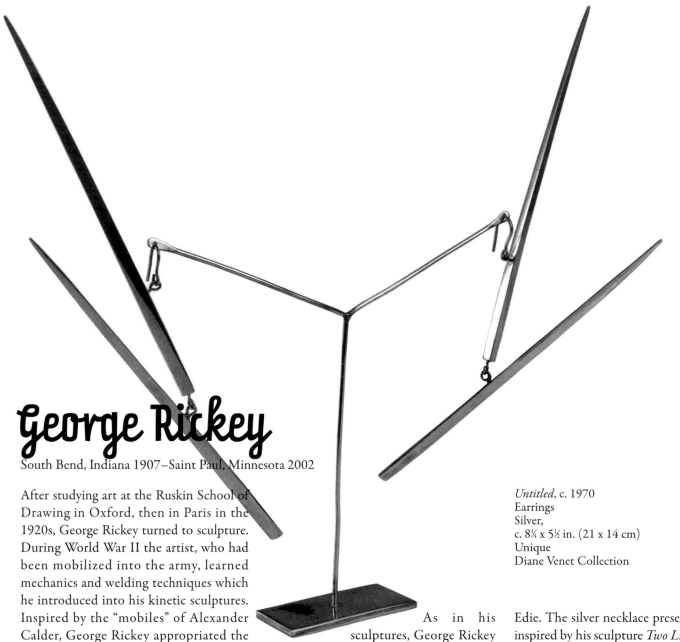

George Rickey

South Bend, Indiana 1907–Saint Paul, Minnesota 2002

After studying art at the Ruskin School of Drawing in Oxford, then in Paris in the 1920s, George Rickey turned to sculpture. During World War II the artist, who had been mobilized into the army, learned mechanics and welding techniques which he introduced into his kinetic sculptures. Inspired by the "mobiles" of Alexander Calder, George Rickey appropriated the notions of movement and time, which he pushed to their paroxysm. The scientific data and the precision of lines allow his sculptures to move in the slightest breath of air without other mechanical elements.

Untitled, c. 1970
Earrings
Silver,
c. 8¼ x 5½ in. (21 x 14 cm)
Unique
Diane Venet Collection

As in his sculptures, George Rickey used stainless steel, occasionally gilded, for the realization of the few necklaces and hairpins that he created. They contain mobile elements and are set on wooden bases, and were made almost exclusively for his wife Edie. The silver necklace presented here is inspired by his sculpture *Two Lines Oblique Down*, a heavy geometrical work produced in 1970. The resemblance between this piece and a wind turbine is characteristic of the artist's attraction for moving shapes derived from a technological vocabulary.

Beverly Pepper

New York 1922–

Beverly Pepper's works are loaded with cultural references. The sculpture *San Martino Altar: Eternal Celebrant* (1992), for instance, borrows its formal vocabulary from that of the Christian altar. She says "What my sculptures consist of, and what they speak about, above all, is timelessness. The future is desire; the past is just a memory. Between these two moments, is an essential position: expectation." In her twenties, Beverly Pepper left the United States and settled in France, where she began her career as a painter studying alongside Fernand Léger and André Lhote; later she went to Italy. Marked by a journey to Cambodia, in 1960 she realized her first wooden sculptures, before going to to make monumental works in Cor-ten steel. Her sculptures gradually transformed into geometrical shapes.

With her mastery of such varying materials as wrought iron and ceramic, Beverly Pepper found it well within her ability to tackle the preparation of a silver necklace. She used rectangular modules, superimposed geometrical forms recalling the disjointed cubes of her sculpture *Perre's Ventaglio III* (1967), whilst preserving a kind of lightness in its almost totemic aspect that becomes apparent when the object is worn. This piece was realized for the curator Jan van der Marck. Beverly Pepper presented her work as a jeweler during the exhibitions Jewelry by Sculptors at the Museum of Modern Art of New York in 1968, then Jewelry as Sculpture as Jewelry at the Institute of Contemporary Art of Boston in 1973.

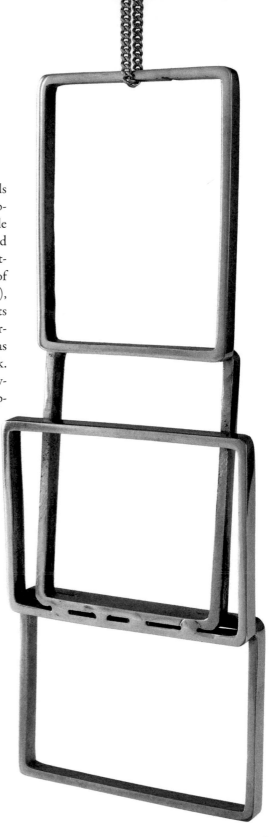

For Jan van der Marck, c. 1970
Necklace
Silver, 3¹⁄₁₆ x 8⅜ x ¹⁄₁₆ in.
(7.75 x 21.25 x 1.75 cm)
Unique
Collection Sheila van der Marck

Jesús Rafael Soto

Ciudad Bolívar 1923–Paris 2005

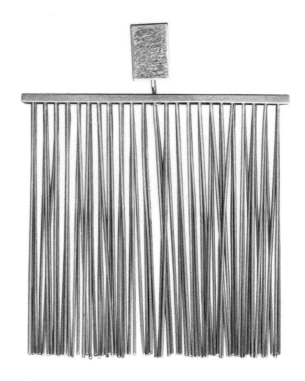

The work of the Venezuelan painter and sculptor Jesús Rafael Soto is characterized by its links with Op Art and kinetic art. He settled in Paris in the 1950s and came to notice for his works using geometrical motifs, arranged in such a way as to obtain visual and vibratory effects. Soto was also interested in the role played by the spectator interacting with his investigations, particularly in the Penetrable series. Today his *Kinetic Murals* can be seen in urban spaces and on the façades of buildings worldwide.

He realized his first jewelry pieces at the end of the 1960s. In 1968, he collaborated with Gem Montebello in the creation of a pair of earrings made from a juxtaposition of gilded silver and silver wires, maintained at their base by a fixed, long silver tube. An illusion of movement is created by an optical phenomenon. Soto creates an interaction between materials and the phenomenon of vibration brought about by the body: the movement of the materials associated with the visual perception of the spectator suggests mobility. This series of jewelry was presented during the exhibitions Multiples: The First Decade in 1971 in Philadelphia, and Jewelry to Sculpture to Jewelry in 1973 in Boston.

Untitled
Earrings
Silver and plated gold,
3³⁄₁₆ x 2¹¹⁄₁₆ in. (9 x 6.8 cm)
Edition Gem GianCarlo Montebello
Diane Venet collection

The brooch *Object Op Art* in painted metal with a silver circumference brings to mind other artists involved in kinetic art—Vasarely, Jean Tinguely, and Yaacov Agam, for example—whose works find echoes in Soto's oeuvre. He began creating a final series of jewelry shortly before his death, producing in association with the Spanish silversmith Chus Burés in 2004, the necklace *Red Balears* using silver and colored enamel, again similar to the visual effects of Op Art.

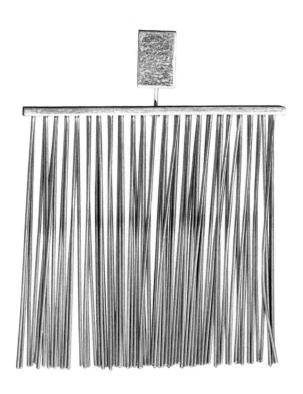

Balears rouge, 2004
Silver and colored metal wire
Private collection

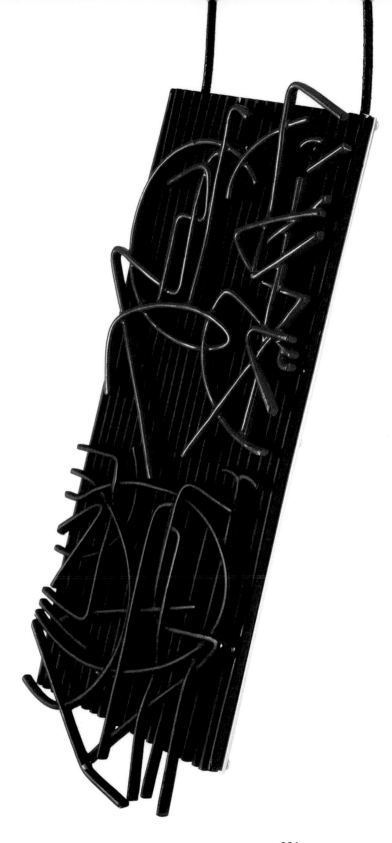

Bernar Venet
Château-Arnoux 1941–

Saturation
Brooch
Silver
Unique
Diane Venet Collection

From his beginnings at the age of nineteen, Bernar Venet has made his mark through radical art acts and through the deployment of materials alien to the artistic practice of his time. A performance in 1961, during which he lay down in refuse, was accompanied by pictures made of tar. In 1963, his "heap of coal," presented as sculpture without specific form, whipped up a scandal before gaining acceptance as a groundbreaking statement. Residing in New York from 1966 to 1970, the oeuvre he developed was based on the language of mathematics, making him one of the pioneers of conceptual art.

After a hiatus, Venet returned to painting, with the thoroughgoing and open-ended exploration of line as its essential subject. His many exhibitions highlight the logic of an evolution in which sculpture has grown to occupy the predominant place and which in time presented the possibility of miniaturization. Knowing it would delight his wife, Venet has amused himself transforming slender gold and silver bars into one-off pieces – rings, bracelets, and pendants – which encapsulate and retrace the development of his output as a sculptor.

Ten Straight Lines, 2000
Pendant
Silver, 5⅛ x 2⅜ in. (13 x 6 cm)
Unique
Diane Venet collection

.../

Random. Combination of Indeterminate Lines, 1992
Necklace
Gold, 2¹⁵⁄₁₆ x 3⅜ in. (7.5 x 8.5 cm)
Unique
Diane Venet collection

Indeterminated line, 2008
Ring
Gold
Unique
Diane Venet collection

Roman Opalka
Hocquincourt 1931–

Roman Opalka is a painter of Polish origin born in France. In 1965, in Warsaw, he was waiting for his wife in a café. She took her time coming, and it was while he was waiting that he found the solution for his work in gestation: he decided to materialize the painting of time. His *Details* are always the same format: the size of the door of his studio in Warsaw, and are covered with a sequence of numbers to represent the passing of time. This work, entitled *1965 / 1 – ∞*, will only be finished upon his death.

When in the late 1970s he met his second wife, Marie-Madeleine, in France, he gave her a gold medal completely covered with engraved numbers. This piece of jewelry remains a one-off piece, and is entitled, as are his paintings: *1965 / 1 – ∞*.

1965/1-∞, c. 1975
Medal necklace
Gold, diameter: 1⁹⁄₁₆ in. (4 cm)
Unique
Marie-Madeleine Opalka collection

Nigel Hall

Bristol 1943–

Nigel Hall creates minimalist works inspired by natural spaces. He often uses wood and steel in the production of geometric forms (lines, arcs, cones, circles, and ellipses). The interplay of shadow and light are also essential in his reinterpretations of moors and hills. His works are often installed in natural environments.

Since the mid-1960s, Nigel Hall has combined sculpted work with drawings which are "related explorations" linked to his concerns and analysis of construction in a defined space. He declares that his work is always conceived in connection with place and placement. Unity is the key word to describe his work, which explores a vast directory of ideas, from bridges to the metaphorical representation of English churches, without ever losing the coherence of its abstract and geometric vocabulary. His consecration arrived in 2003 when the sculptor was elected a member of the Royal Academy of Arts.

In 2009, he created a gold brooch issued in edition of seven copies, entitled *Snow Light*. This piece of jewelry is an exact reproduction of the sculpture of the same name, realized in 2004, in which he elaborated a game of shadow and light, which penetrates alternately into the spherical recesses of the wood.

Snow Light, 2009
Brooch
Silver,
2⅝ x 2⅝ x ⅜ in. (6.7 x 6.7 x 1 cm)
Edition of 7
Nigel Hall collection

Keith Sonnier

Mamou, Louisiana 1941–

The work of Keith Sonnier is linked to the "new sculpture" of the 1960s, in the same way as the works of Richard Serra, Bruce Nauman, and Richard Tuttle. The artist uses uncommon materials such as latex, bamboo, satellite transmitters, cheesecloth, flocking, lost property, or video in minimalist compositions. From 1968 onward, neon was to take a more dominating place in his work, and he used it in the making of lamps, jewelry, and sculpture, as a material capable of interacting with space and the surrounding colors. An important element of his work is its relation to the space where it is shown, rather than a space within a frame. Such is the case of his piece *Dis-Play II*, an imposing installation made of many different materials including foam, glass, strobes, and fluorescent pigments that allow the artist to treat light and space as both tactile materials and also optical devices.

The necklace *Flower of Life*, made in 2009, is typical of his work in its use of neon and the perfect simplicity of its shape.

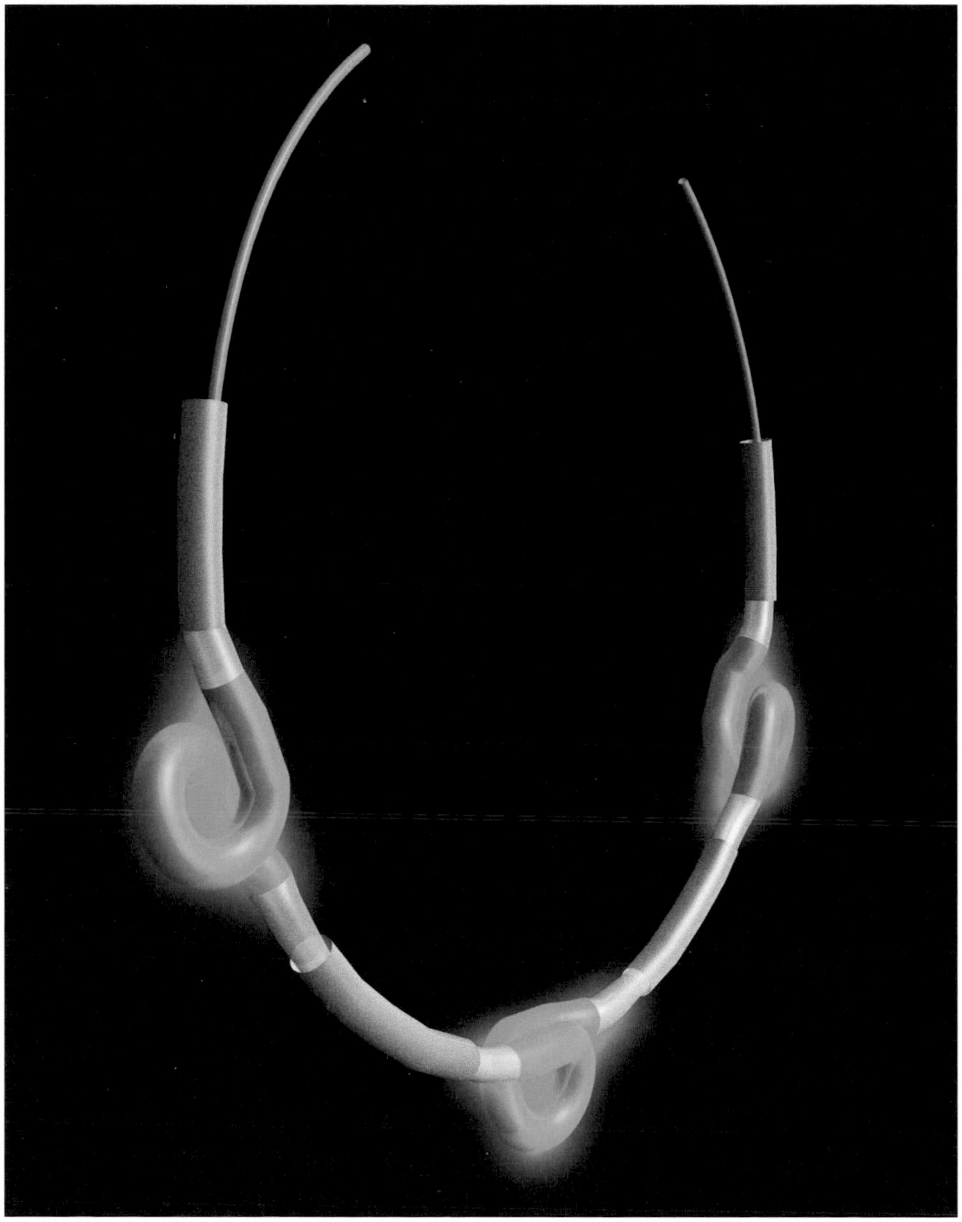

Flower of Life, 2009
Necklace
Neon, plastic,
11¹³⁄₁₆ x 7¹⁄₁₆ in. (30 x 18 cm)
Unique
Keith Sonnier collection

And also...

Valerio Adami Bologna 1935–
Diamond. A World Photographie,
1989, brooch
Yellow, white and pink gold and
diamonds, 2⅜ x 2 ⁹⁄₁₆ x ⁹⁄₁₆ in.
(6 x 6.5 x 1.5 cm)
Edition Arent e Van Leeum
Marina Filippini collection

Richard Tuttle New Jersey 1941–
Amber Necklace, 1995
Necklace
Amber, gold, Italian coral, jade, jet,
platinum, pearls, silk and white gold,
5¼ x 1¹⁵⁄₁₆ in. (13.3 x 5 cm)
Artist's collection

Ron Arad Tel-Aviv 1951–
Hot Ingo Earrings, 2007
Earrings
White polyamide and platinum,
3¹⁵⁄₁₆ x 1 x 1 in. (10 x 2.5 x 2.5 cm)
Edition of 100, artist's studio
Diane Venet collection

Stephen Antonakos Laconia 1926–
Untitled, 1991, Brooch
Gold and silver,
1½ x 1¹⁄₁₆ in. (3.75 x 2.7 cm)
Unique
Naomi Antonakos collection

Arnaldo Pomodoro
Morciano di Romagna 1926–
Untitled, 1967, necklace, silver,
18⅛ in. (46 cm), Edition of 200,
Gem GianCarlo Montebello,
Diane Venet collection

DeWain Valentine
Fort Collins 1936–
Untitled, 1987, pendant, glass,
2⅟₁₆ x 2⅟₁₆ (5.2 x 5.,2 cm),
unique
Diane Venet collection

Sophia Vari
Athens 1940–
Helios
Ring

Kiki Smith
Nuremberg 1954–
Bright
Pendant

Bernar Venet
Château-Arnoux 1951–
Indeterminate Line, 1998
Ring, silver
Unique
Diane Venet collection

Laura Ford Cardiff 1961–
Head in the clouds, 2008
Brooch, silver and enamel paint,
1¹⁵⁄₁₆ x 2⅜ in. (5 x 6 cm)
2/7
Laura Ford collection

Marie Noëlle de la Poype
Untitled, c. 2000
Pendant,
cetacean bones and paint
Pierre-Alain Challier collection

.../

231

...And also...

Pol Bury
Haine-Saint-Pierre 1922
–Paris 2005
Untitled,
Ring

Beat Zoderer
Zurich 1955–
*14 Crayons on
14Wires*, 2006
Necklace, Mini
crayons and wire,
Unique,
Margareta
von Bartha
collection

Ben Naples 1935–
Je me sens libre, 2001
Bracelet
Silver,
1½ x 2¹³⁄₁₆ x 2 ⁵⁄₁₆ in.
(3.9 x 7.1 x 5.9 cm)
4/8
Filippini collection

James Brown
Los Angeles 1951–
California Sea Shells
Necklace
Artist's collection

Pol Bury Haine-Saint-Pierre
1922–Paris 2005
Untitled, Bracelet
Gold, 1⁹⁄₁₆ x 2¾ in. (4 x 7 cm)
Edition, Gem GianCarlo
Montebello
Diane Venet collection

Lynda Benglis Louisana 1941–
Untitled, brooch, Silver,
1 x 1 x 2¼ in.
(2.5 x 12 x 5.7 cm),
unique
Sara and Marc
Brenda
collection

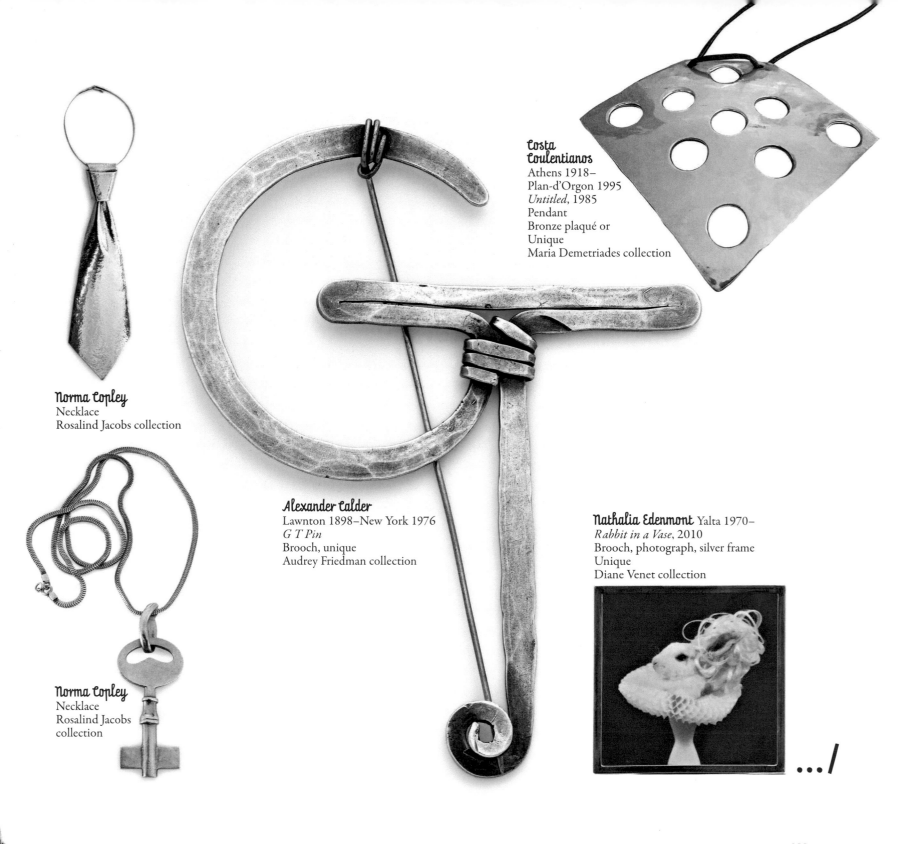

Norma Copley
Necklace
Rosalind Jacobs collection

Norma Copley
Necklace
Rosalind Jacobs
collection

Alexander Calder
Lawnton 1898–New York 1976
G T Pin
Brooch, unique
Audrey Friedman collection

Costa Coulentianos
Athens 1918–
Plan-d'Orgon 1995
Untitled, 1985
Pendant
Bronze plaqué or
Unique
Maria Demetriades collection

Nathalia Edenmont Yalta 1970–
Rabbit in a Vase, 2010
Brooch, photograph, silver frame
Unique
Diane Venet collection

.../

233

.../And also...

Max Ernst Brülh 1891–Paris 1976
Égyptienne, brooch
Gold, 3⁵⁄₁₆ x 2¹⁵⁄₁₆ in. (8,4 x 7,4 cm)
7/8, François Hugo
Diana Küppers collection

Alberto Guzmán Piura 1927–
Mobile, 2006, Ring
Gold, 1 x 1³⁄₁₆
        (2,5 x 3 cm), unique
    Naïla de Montbrison
    collection

Anish Kapoor Bombay 1954–
Untitled, 2008
Necklace
Diane Venet collection

Bruno Martinazzi Turin 1923–
Hand
Bracelet

Fausto Melotti,
Trent 1901–Milan 1986
Moon
Earrings
Diane Venet collection

Ruth Francken Prague 1924–Paris 2006
Bust Lilith, 1974
Brooch
Diana Küppers collection

Marisol Escobar
Paris 1930–
Self Portrait, 1967
Ring
Bill Katz
collection

Forrest Myers Hawaï 1941–
Wire Bracelet, 2008
Bracelet
Sara and Marc Benda collection

David Nash
England 1945–
Brooch
Christian Scheffel Gallery
collection

Tim Noble and Sue Wester
Stroud 1966– and Leicester 1967–
Fucking Beautiful, 2004
Necklace
Diane Venet collection

Fabrizio Plessi, Reggio Emilia 1940–
The Soul Light, 2006, necklace
Diane Venet collection

Michele Oka Doner
Florida 1945–
Coral Reef Bracelet, 2007
Bracelet
Sara and Marc Benda collection

Vassilakis Takis Athens 1925–
Untitled, c. 1980
Gold with detachable magnetic
beads, c. 4¾ in. (12 cm)
Bracelet
Maria Demetriades collection

235

Bibliography

GENERAL WORKS

CERVAL Marguerite de, *Dictionnaire international du bijou*, Paris: Éditions du Regard, 1998

CLARKE Beccy and Indigo Clarke, *New direction in Jewellery II*, London: Black Dog Publishing, 2006

FARNETI CERA Deanna, *L'art du bijou*, Paris: Flammarion, 1992

GRANET Danièle and LAMOUR Catherine, *Grands et petits secrets du monde de l'art*, Paris: Fayard, 2010

GUADALUPI Gianni, *Ors et trésors – Chefs-d'œuvre de joaillerie de l'antiquité à nos jours*, Paris: Éditions White Star, 2008

ST CLAIR Temple, *Alchemy: a passion for jewels*, New York: Harper Collins Publishers, 2008

WALTHER Ingo F., (dir.), *L'art au XXe siècle*, Cologne: Taschen, 2005

SPECIALIST PUBLICATIONS

BALDWIN James and GIROUD Françoise, *César, compressions d'or*, Paris: Hachette, 1973

BIZOT C., *Catherine Noll*, Editions du Regard, Paris: 2001

RATEAU Armand-Albert, *Picasso et l'atelier Hugo 1953–1971*, Paris: Vallois, 1989

Dali joie-bijou, Turin: Umberto Allemandi, 2001

DORMER Peter and TURNER Ralph, *The New Jewelry: Trends and Traditions*, London: Thames & Hudson, 1985

GABARDI Melissa, *Jean Després maestra orafo tra art déco e avangardie*, Milan: Idea Books, 1999

GABARDI Melissa, *Les bijoux des années 50*, Paris: Éditions de l'amateur, 1987

JORIS Yvonne, *Private passion. Artists' Jewelry of the 20th century*, Stuttgart: Arnoldsche Art Publishers, 2009

MARCADÉ Jean-Claude, *Calder, Tout l'art*, Paris: Flammarion, 1996

NEWBY-HASPESLAGH Martine, *Sculpture to wear. Jewellery by post-war painters and sculptors*, Didier Antique, 2010

PAHLKE Rosemarie, *Pol Bury*, Crédit Communal, 1988

PURCELL Katherine, *Falize: A Dynasty of Jewelers*, London: Thames & Hudson, 1999

RAULET Sylvie, *Bijoux Art déco*, Paris: Éditions du Regard, 1984

RAULET Sylvie, *Bijoux des années 1940–1950*, Paris: Éditions du Regard, 1987

RONSIN Albert, *Le trésor des bijoux de Braque*, Paris: Art International Publishers, 1995

SIAUD Claire and HUGO Pierre, *Bijoux d'artistes*, Aix-en-Provence: Les Cyprès Éditeur, 2001

WATKIN David, *The Best in Contemporary Jewellery*, Mies: Rotovision SA, 1993

EXHIBITION CATALOGUES

HUGO Monique et Pierre, *Bijoux d'artistes: Arp, Cocteau, Derain, Ernst, Picasso, Tanning*, Aix en Provence, 1990

BIZOT Chantal, GUIGON Emmanuel, DEVEZE Laurent, *Bijoux d'artistes*, Paris: Hazan, Besançon, musée du Temps, 2009

EIDELBERG Martin et GREENBAUM Toni, *Les messagers du modernisme: bijoux artistiques aux États-Unis de 1940 à 1960*, Paris: Flammarion, Musée des arts décoratifs de Montréal, 1996

Bijoux de lumière de Jacques Gautier, Paris: Union centrale des Arts Décoratifs, 1999

Les bijoux de Torun, Paris: Union central des Arts Décoratifs, 1992

IIIe triennale du bijou, Paris: Edition du May, Union centrale des Arts Décoratifs 1992

ABADIE Daniel, *César: "compressions,"* Knokke-Heist, Christian Fayt Art Gallery, 1983

Bijoux d'artistes, Paris: Galerie Sven, 1976

INGBERG Henry, *Être ou ne pas être... Peintres ou sculpteurs? Les bijoux des plus grands*, Domaine du Château de Seneffe, 2003

JONEMANN Gilles et GARGAT Henri, *Gargat: exposition au musée des arts décoratifs de Paris:* Paris: Union central des Arts Décoratifs, 1988

KAMIL, *Bijoux d'artistes*, Galerie du Forum-Kamil, Monaco, 2005

KROGSGAARD Michael, *Il était une fois un orfèvre... Georg Jensen*, Paris: Maison du Danemark, 2004

KÜPPERS Diana, *Künstlerschmuck Objets d'Art*, Hirmer Verlag, 2009

MATHEY François, *Antagonismes 2: l'Objet*, Paris: Tournon, 1962

MOLINS Javier et BARANANO Kosme de, *Joyas del arte moderno*, Torrent, Emate, 2009

MOSCO Marilena, *L'arte del gioiello e il gioiello d'artista dal 900 ad oggi*, Florence, Museo degli Argenti, 2001

VENET Diane, *Bijoux sculptures: l'art vous va si bien*, Paris: Gallimard, Roubaix, La piscine musée d'art et d'industrie André Diligent, 2008

Magazines

BOUGAULT Valérie, "Bijoux Art Déco & avant-garde, Jean Després et les bijoux modernes," *Connaissance des arts*, Hors série n°398, 2009

BRUNHAMMER Yvonne, "René Lalique, bijoux d'exception 1890-1912," *Beaux Arts Magazine*, Hors-série, 2007

CHAMPENOIS Michèle, "Talismans d'artistes," *Le Monde*, 3 mai 2008, p. 30–33

COLLECTIF, "Ils veulent rénover l'art du bijou," *Connaissance des arts* n°108, February 1961, p. 30–37

COLLECTIF, "Ces femmes qui ont révolutionné l'art," *Connaissance des Arts* n°658, March 2008, p. 50–59

CONTI Samantha, "Home front: At Louisa Guinness's London furniture gallery, a bold new design movement is brewing," *W Magazine*, March 2004

CROWLE A., "Artists with a jewel purpose," *The Daily Telegraph*, November 25, 2003

ERNOULD-GANDOUET Marielle, "Sur un nu de Maillol les bijoux d'artistes," *L'Estampille* n° 39, Febuary 1973, p. 43–46

GRAINVILLE Patrick, "Bijoux d'artistes," *L'Œil* n° 353, December 1984, p. 52–56

JULIUS Corinne, "Past and Present: Jewellery by 20th Century Artists," *World Interiors*, December 2003

REARDON Kate, "Jewellery, art, whatever, it's decorative as hell and about the coolest thing you can wear," *Times Weekend*, February 2004, p. 53

Sales Catalogues

SVV ADER, PICARD, *Bijoux d'artistes, sculptures, peintures*, Paris: Hôtel Drouot, sale of May 29, 1990

SVV ARTCURIAL, *Bijoux d'artistes: Lalanne, Delaunay, Berrocal, Sanchez, Pomodoro, Takis, Arman: catalogue et prix*, Paris: Artcurial, February 2008

SVV CHARBONNEAUX, *Bijoux et créations d'artistes*, Paris: Hôtel Drouot, sale of November 25, 1990

SVV CHARBONNEAUX Catherine, *Bijoux anciens et modernes, collection de bijoux d'artistes, argenterie*, Paris: Hôtel Drouot, sale of May 31, 2007

SVV CHARBONNEAUX Catherine, *Bijoux anciens et modernes, collection de bijoux d'artistes, argenterie*, Paris: Hôtel Drouot, sale of May 30, 2008

SVV CHARBONNEAUX Catherine, *Bijoux anciens et modernes, bijoux d'artistes et de créateurs, argenterie*, Paris: Hôtel Drouot, sale of April 8, 2009

SVV CHORRON-BARRE ALLARDI, *Amateurs et collections XV: estampes, gravures lithographies, bijoux d'artistes, ensemble d'œuvre sur papier*, Paris: Hôtel Drouot, sale of February 6, 2009

SVV DEURAUX-APONEM, *Bijoux d'artistes collection Robert Goossens*, Paris: Hôtel Drouot, sale of February 18, 2008

SVV HOEBANKS & COUTURIER, *Bijoux d'artistes... Objets d'artistes*, Paris: Hôtel Drouot, sale of November 19, 1989

SVV HOEBANKS & COUTURIER, *Bijoux d'artistes... Objets d'artistes*, Paris: Hôtel Drouot, sale of February 12, 1989

SVV HOEBANKS & COUTURIER, *Bijoux d'artistes... Objets d'artistes*, Paris: Hôtel Drouot, sale of March 17, 1991

SVV HOEBANKS & COUTURIER, *Bijoux d'artistes... Objets d'artistes*, Paris: Hôtel Drouot, sale of November 17, 1991

SVV HOEBANKS & COUTURIER, *Bijoux d'artistes... Objets d'artistes*, Paris: Hôtel Drouot, sale of April 5, 1992

SVV HOEBANKS & COUTURIER, *Bijoux d'artistes... Objets d'artistes*, Paris: Hôtel Drouot, sale of November 29, 1992

SVV HOEBANKS & COUTURIER, *Bijoux d'artistes... Objets d'artistes*, Paris: Hôtel Drouot, sale of April 4, 1993

SVV ROBERT & BAILLE, *Bijoux de haute couture, costume jewelry & bijoux de haute fantaisie, bijoux d'artistes*, Paris: Hôtel Drouot, sale of March 19, 2007

SVV ROBERT & BAILLE, *Bijoux de haute couture, costume jewelry & bijoux de haute fantaisie, bijoux d'artistes*, Paris: Hôtel Drouot, sale of March 30, 2008

SVV ROBERT & BAILLE, *Bijoux de haute couture, bijoux de haute fantaisie, bijoux d'artistes 1930-2009*, Paris: Hôtel Drouot, sale of November 16, 2009

SVV ROBERT & BAILLE, *Bijoux de haute couture, costume jewelry & bijoux de haute fantaisie, bijoux d'artistes*, Paris: Hôtel Drouot, sale of June 15, 2009

SVV TAJAN, *Mobilier & bijoux d'artistes*, Paris: Tajan, sale of November 19, 2008

SVV TAJAN, *Mobilier & bijoux d'artistes*, Paris: Tajan, sale of March 16, 2010

Websites

www.dianevenet.com

www.louisaguinnessgallery.com

www.daliparis.com

www.armanstudio.com

Index

A

ABAKANOWICZ,
Magdalena
117

ADAMI,
Valerio
230

ANTONAKOS,
Stephen
230

APPEL,
Karel
178

ARAD,
Ron
230

ARMAN,
160, 161, 162, 163

ARP,
Jean (Hans)
92, 93

ATTIA,
Kader
175

B

BAJ,
Enrico
179

BALLA,
Giacomo
51

BARCELÓ,
Miquel
122, 123

BEN,
232

BENGLIS,
Lynda
232

BERTOIA,
Harry
46, 47

BLOCH,
Pierrette
208

BOURGEOIS,
Louise
124, 125, 126, 127

BRAQUE,
Georges
31, 32, 33

BROWN,
James
209, 232

BURY,
Pol
180, 232

C

CALDER,
Alexander
40, 41, 42, 43, 44, 45,
233

CARO,
Antony
210, 211

CÉSAR,
152, 153, 154, 155

CHAMBERLAIN,
John
157

CHAPMAN,
Dinos
174

CHEVALIER
Miguel,
150

CHILLIDA
Eduardo
69

CHIRICO
Giorgio De
73

COCTEAU
Jean
94, 95

COPLEY,
Norma
233

CORNEILLE,
147

COULENTIANOS,
Costas
59, 233

CRAIG-MARTIN,
Michael
151

D

DALÍ,
Salvador
78, 79, 80

DELVOYE,
Wim
128

DERAIN,
André
28, 29

E

ENDEMONT,
Nathalia
233

ERNST,
Max
74, 75, 76, 77, 234

ESCOBAR,
Marisol
234

ÉTIENNE-MARTIN,
Henri
50

F

FINI,
Leonor
88, 89

FONTANA,
Lucio
204, 205, 206, 207

FORD,
Laura
231

FRANCKEN,
Ruth
234

G

GARGALLO,
Pablo
49

GIACOMETTI
Alberto
54, 55

GONZÁLEZ
Julio
63

GUZMAN
Alberto
129, 234

H

HAINS
Raymond
168

HALL,
Nigel
228

HARING,
Keith
177

HIRST,
Damien
119

HOLZER,
Jenny
131

D'HUART,
Annabelle
110

HUNTER,
Kenny
115

I

INDIANA,
Robert
169

K

KABAKOV,
Ilya
108

KAPOOR,
Anish
215, 234

KLASEN,
Peter
176

KLEIN,
Yves
183

KOONS,
Jeff
185

KOSICE,
Gyula
130

KUSAMA,
Yayoi
186, 187

L

LALANE,
Claude
111, 112, 113

LAM,
Wilfredo
98, 99

LEBEL,
Jean-Jacques
201

LÉGER,
Fernand
52, 53

LICHTENSTEIN,
Roy
172, 173,

LIPSCHITZ,
Jacques
100, 101

M

MAGRITTE,
René
102, 103

MAN RAY,
83, 84, 85, 86, 87

MARTINAZZI,
Bruno
234

MATHIEU,
Georges
132

MATTA,
Roberto
90, 91

MELOTTI,
Fausto
234

MINJUN,
Yue
133

MIYAJIMA,
Tatsuo
189

MONORY,
Jacques
200

MORELLET,
François
214

MYERS,
Forrest
235

N

NASH,
David
235

NESBITT,
Lowell
146

NEVELSON,
Louise
134, 135

NOBLE,
Tim
121, 235

O

OKA DONER,
Michel
235

ONO,
Yoko
193

OPALKA,
Roman
226

OPPENHEIM,
Meret
190, 191

ORLAN,
136

P

PAIK,
Nam June
194

PENONE,
Giuseppe
109

PEPPER,
Beverly
219

PERRY,
Grayson
188

PICASSO,
Pablo
35, 37, 36, 38, 39

PLENSA,
Jaume
217

PLESSI,
Fabrizio
235

POIRIER,
Anne et Patrick
137

POMODORO,
Arnaldo
56, 57, 231

POMODORO,
Gio
58

POYPE
Marie Noëlle de la,
231

Q

QUINN
Marc
106, 107

QUINZE,
Arne
195

R

RAUSCHENBERG,
Robert
196, 197

RICKEY,
George
218

ROTELLA,
Mimmo
181

S

SAINT-PHALLE,
Niki de
164, 165, 166, 167

SAMARAS,
Lucas
138, 139

SCHARF,
Kenny
159

SEVERINI,
Gino
48

SMITH,
Kiki
141, 231

SONNIER,
Keith
229

SOTO
Jesus Rafael
220

SPOERRI
Daniel,
114

STELLA,
Frank
142, 143

SULTAN,
Donald
199

T

TAKIS,
60, 61, 235

TANNING,
Dorothea
96, 97

TASTSIOGLOU,
Nakis
144

TAYLOR-WOOD,
Sam
145

TUNGA,
140

TURK,
Gavin
120

TUTTLE,
Richard
230

U

UECKER,
Günther
184

V

VALENTINE,
DeWain
231

VARI,
Sophia
231

VASARELY,
Victor
65

VENET,
Bernar
222, 223, 224, 225, 231

VILLEGLÉ,
Jacques
158

W

WARHOL,
Andy
170

WEBSTER,
Sue
121, 235

WIRKKALA,
Tapio
66, 67

LEWITT,
Sol
213

Y

YOUNGERMAN,
Jack
192

Z

ZODERER,
Beat
232

EDITORIAL
DIRECTION
Julie Rouart
assisted by Camille Giordano

DESIGN
Susanna Shannon
+Tom Caïani/ design dept.

NOTES
ABOUT THE ARTISTS
Delphine Séïté

TRANSLATED FROM THE
FRENCH
Text by Adrien Goetz
David Radzinowicz
Notes about the artists
Plum Le Tan

PROOFREADING
Helen Woodhall

PRODUCTION
Corinne Trovarelli

COLOR
SEPARATION
Articrom, Milano

PRINTING
Gruppo Editoriale Zanardi, Italy

ISBN
978-88-572-1156-5

©SKIRA, 2011